A HAMPSHIRE MANOR

The village of Hinton Ampner lies in an unspoilt sweep of chalk countryside, a cluster of cottages round the parish church and the manor house. Until it came to the National Trust in 1986, the Hampshire estate of Hinton Ampner had been in the hands of the Stewkeley, Stawell and Dutton families for nearly 400 years. This delightful account of the history of the house and the people connected with it was written by the 8th and last Lord Sherborne, who completely remodelled the unattractive Victorian mansion he inherited and created the magnificent garden. The house is typical of countless smaller country houses in which the quality of life was in many ways more enviable than that in the greater houses. The book describes the village and the countryside in which it lies, the history of the occupants of the Manor House, the various architectural transformation which it has undergone since the end of the eighteenth century, and the development of the garden and the planting of the park.

Ralph Dutton, the 8th and last Lord Sherborne, died in 1985 at the age of 86. He generously bequeathed the house of Hinton Ampner and its estate to the National Trust, after a lifetime devoted to executing his vision for it. He worked at the College of Arms and at Lloyd's. He wrote a number of witty and erudite books and served on committees of the National Trust and the National Art-Collections Fund, and as a trustee of the Wallace Collection.

Lydia Greeves is a freelance editor and writer with a particular interest in cultural history. She is currently working on a new edition of *The National Trust Guide*.

Cover painting shows the *Entrance Front of Hinton Ampner,* by Matthew Rice.

A Hampshire Manor
HINTON AMPNER

Ralph Dutton

Introduction by Lydia Greeves

CENTURY
LONDON MELBOURNE AUCKLAND JOHANNESBURG

First published in 1968 by B.T. Batsford Ltd

This edition first published in 1988 by Century, an imprint of
Century Hutchinson Ltd, in association with The National Trust
for Places of Historic Interest or Natural Beauty, 36 Queen Anne's
Gate, London SW1H 9AS

Century Hutchinson Ltd, Brookmount House, 62-65 Chandos Place,
London WC2N 4NW

Century Hutchinson Australia Pty Ltd,
PO Box 496, 16-22 Church Street, Hawthorn, Melbourne,
Victoria 3122, Australia

Century Hutchinson Group New Zealand Limited,
PO Box 40-086, Glenfield, Auckland 10, New Zealand

Century Hutchinson South Africa (Pty) Ltd,
PO Box 337, Bergvlei, 2012 South Africa

Dutton, Ralph, *1898-1985*
   A Hampshire manor: Hinton Ampner.
   - (National Trust classics).
   1. Hampshire. Hinton Ampner. Manors
   I. Title   II. Series
   942.2'75

   ISBN 0-7126-1790-6

Published in association with The National Trust, this series
is devoted to reprinting books on the artistic, architectural,
social and cultural heritage of Britain. The imprint
covers buildings and monuments, arts and crafts, gardening and
landscape in a variety of literary forms, including histories,
memoirs, biographies and letters.

The Century Classics also include the Travellers, Seafarers and
Lives and Letters series.

Printed in Great Britain by Richard Clay Ltd., Bungay, Suffolk.

Contents

Introduction to this Edition

⚬⌇⌇⌇⌇⌇⌇⌇⌇⌇

Ralph Dutton, the 8th and last Lord Sherborne, died in 1985 at the age of 86 after a fall at his house at Hinton Ampner. He bequeathed his estate to the National Trust and both house and garden are now open to the public. Some 17 years before he died he wrote this account of the place he loved and in which he had spent his childhood. It is a portrait of a corner of rural England and of the people connected with it, but unlike so many other country communities now swallowed up by urban development, or taken over by weekenders, Hinton Ampner still retains its essential character. Only 8 miles east of Winchester and with Southampton and Portsmouth a mere 20 miles or so to the south, the little village lies in an unspoilt sweep of chalk countryside, a cluster of cottages round parish church and manor house. To visit it today is to recapture the England of Thomas Hardy and William Cobbett and to imagine for an afternoon that you have left the twentieth century behind.

Ralph Dutton's house and garden maintain this illusion. Although both are creations of the mid-twentieth century, and are of importance for this alone, they seem rooted in the past, part of a historical continuum reaching back to the Middle Ages and forward into the future. This sense of timelessness, of a building and its setting as part of the landscape, owes much to the vision and sense of history of Ralph Dutton himself. The estate he inherited from his father had been successively in the hands of the Stewkeley, Stawell and Dutton families for nearly four hundred years, but the haunted Tudor manor house which once stood here was demolished in 1793, its site now marked by the orchard beside the church, and the Georgian house then built to the south was encased in a gabled Victorian shell and much enlarged by Ralph Dutton's grandparents. The garden too reflected Victorian taste, with numerous borders and five large greenhouses to provide flowers for the house, and an old-fashioned and unsuccessful rose garden which needed replanting every two years or so. Ralph Dutton's father had no interest in the garden and was unwilling to countenance alterations to something which he considered unnecessary. His artistic mother would have made changes if she had been allowed to, and she was responsible for the balustrade to the south of the house which frames the view from the principal rooms.

Today the sense of unity in the garden is striking. With the help of his head gardeners, Walter Holloway and, subsequently, Herbert Gray, Ralph Dutton created a series of garden 'rooms' of varying shape and perspective, all individual in character, but contributing to a coherent whole. Part of the charm of the place lies in the numerous changes of level, often linked by brick steps which have now mellowed to a pleasing rusty red. And yet the garden is not closed in upon itself, but shades easily into the park and countryside beyond. From the broad terrace in front of the house there is no other building to be seen in the great sweep of Hampshire before you. At harvest time, the ochre of the stubble fields sets off the dark green foliage of the trees in the park. In the foreground a flight of brick steps leads to the sunken garden, the stone balustrades on either side covered in yellow lichen. The whole is a composition in the English tradition of landscape gardening, a vision translated into reality. When he first inherited, Ralph Dutton planted several hundred trees in the park and on the hills beyond to soften the hard lines of the fields in the distant views from the house. The remains of an old lime avenue, part of the Tudor layout, were cleverly linked to the garden by a grass walk on the same axis. Pairs of Irish yews flanking the Long Walk exaggerate its length and frame a vista into the park at one end. When this walk was planted, the yews were only two feet high; it is we who have benefited from one man's faith in the future.

The house too shows the same delight in proportion and effect, with everything in it chosen and placed in accordance with Ralph Dutton's admiration for the taste of the Regency period. He remodelled the Victorian house, creating a Georgian building in warm red brick, now clothed in magnolia, honeysuckle and other climbing plants. Eighteenth-century fittings were acquired from houses in London and the country that had been, or were being, demolished, and Hinton was filled with a distinguished collection of furniture and *objets d'art*, supplemented by decorative paintings that reflected his interest in Italian seventeenth-century painting. When the house was almost completely destroyed by fire in April 1960, Ralph Dutton immediately set about rebuilding it and refurnishing it as beautifully as before.

If Ralph Dutton had lived two or three hundred years ago, he would not have been remarkable, but for a man who reached adulthood as the First World War ended, his achievements are impressive; with his great knowledge of architecture, interior decoration and gardens he was a true connoisseur and one of the last of his kind. Although his father had longed for a son, he took little interest in Ralph as a boy, regretting his lack of enthusiasm for hunting, shooting and other sporting activities. It was his mother who arranged his education, sending him first to West Downs Preparatory School near Winchester, then under its first headmaster. She was a major influence on her son and from her he inherited his artistic nature. She was musical, a painter and an accomplished linguist, speaking French, German, Spanish and Italian fluently. Even as a small boy, Ralph showed considerable interest in architecture and would spend hours designing imaginary houses. He too was a linguist, and many of the books he bought for the library to replace those lost in the fire were French.

After preparatory school Ralph followed in his father's footsteps to Eton and then spent a year at Christ Church, Oxford. This was one of the happiest periods of his life and at Oxford he made many friends who were to remain close in the years that followed. While at Oxford he formed the Uffizi Society and invited eminent speakers from the artistic world to address it. He once showed a photograph of this small group, whose members included Lord David Cecil and Lord Holden, with whom he was later to write a book, to his father, who is said to have remarked that he would have preferred to see a picture of a cricket eleven.

Oxford was followed by a course at Cirencester Agricultural College and then, until he inherited Hinton Ampner in 1935, Ralph Dutton lived and worked in London, first at the College of Arms and then at Lloyd's. Even when established in Hampshire, he continued to spend the week in London at his flat in Eaton Square, which he furnished as beautifully as his house. In London, until his sight failed, he led a sociable life, returning every weekend to the peace of his beloved Hinton. He was a frequent visitor to horticultural shows, ordering plants on the spot if he saw something he liked.

Some of his collection was bought at auction and some from London dealers, but many of his finer pieces and pictures were bought on his travels abroad, particularly in France and Italy. He loved Venice and went there every year, staying with his friends Mr and Mrs Paul Wallraff, who would accompany him on his visits to the city's galleries. When in Italy he was also often the guest of Sir Osbert Sitwell at Montegufoni. Nearly all the pictures at Hinton Ampner were Italian landscapes of the seventeenth and eighteenth centuries, but to his great sadness three of the best, as well as some family miniatures, were taken in a burglary and have never been recovered. In his purchases for the house, as in his remodelling of the garden, Ralph Dutton showed a remarkable ability to carry a vision of what he wanted in his head. Every picture and every piece of furniture was bought for a particular position and nothing was ever found to be unsuitable for its planned location. He was fond of hardstones and in particular of porphyry and bluejohn. A giltwood side-table in the drawing-room with a top of white marble and bluejohn was once in Lord Curzon's house in Carlton House Terrace and was bought by Ralph Dutton with the fee of £100 earned from his book *The English Country House*, first published in 1935. And it would have given him great pleasure to have known that his ormolu bluejohn perfume-burner, a purchase of which he was especially proud, was to be one of the pieces selected to represent the work of Matthew Boulton at the *Treasure Houses of Britain* exhibition held in Washington in 1985.

Later in life Ralph Dutton's knowledge and experience benefited several national institutions and charities. He was a Trustee of the Wallace Collection from 1948 to 1969 and a member of the Executive Committee of the National Art-Collections Fund from 1952 to 1970. He also served on committees of the National Trust, while he was generally best known for his many witty and authoritative books on architecture, internal decoration and travel. He loved to show visitors his house and garden and was host to many parties from abroad, particularly from America and France. His garden was opened each year under the National Gardens Scheme and in aid of the Red Cross and other charities.

Distinguished visitors to Hinton Ampner included his friends Sir Osbert and Sacheverell Sitwell, the Husseys of Scotney and Rudyard Kipling's son-in-law and daughter Elsie, Captain and Mrs George Bambridge, who bequeathed Wimpole Hall in Cambridgeshire to the Trust. The pleasure of staying in a house full of beautiful things must have been enhanced by the fact that Ralph Dutton's appreciation of the finer things in life extended to the soap and the linen; and the cooking of his housekeeper Mrs Cross was superb. Afternoon tea was not served when the master was alone at Hinton, as he preferred to be out walking on the estate, but Mrs Cross would always bake one of her magnificent cakes for his guests.

As the patron of the living, Ralph Dutton took a paternal interest in the welfare of the little parish church. He was not a deeply religious man and never took Communion, but he attended services, often read the lesson on Sunday and did much to improve and beautify the modest nineteenth-century building that lay only a few paces from his front door.

Among other alterations, he replaced glazed Victorian tiles by the present stone floor. He also commissioned the striking stained-glass windows from Patrick Reyntiens, one a tongue of flame, the other a study in blue and grey, representing the pillars of fire and cloud which led the Israelites out of Egypt. When *A Hampshire Manor* was written, the family vault in the church had not been discovered (see page 27), but in 1969, when a new heating system was being installed and improvements made to the flooring of the chancel, the steps leading down to the vault were found just in front of the altar rails. Ralph and his sister Joane went into the vault, which was found to contain a large number of coffins of the Stewkeley and Stawell families. Some were very grand, covered in velvet and studded with nails, and at least one bore a coronet; others had disintegrated. Exposure to the air began to cause further deterioration, so the vault was resealed and is now marked by a circle of porphyry in front of the altar. It was also by his initiative that the handsome seventeenth-century family wall monuments were moved to Hinton Ampner Church from the disused and decaying church of St Mary at Laverstoke near Whitchurch.

Ralph Dutton's ashes lie in the old churchyard, a stone's throw from the garden he made and loved. Neither he nor his sisters had married and although he was a man who rarely showed his feelings, his friends knew the strength of his desire to ensure the survival of the Hinton estate after him. Some years before he died he wrote to the National Trust to say that he had decided to bequeath to it his house, most of its contents and his estate, expressing the wish that the estate should be retained intact for as long as possible. In doing so he demonstrated the generosity and modesty that was characteristic of him and also his faith in an organization in whose purposes he believed deeply and with which he had been for so long associated. It is impossible to know now what was in his heart, but his memorial, let into the floor of the chancel in the little church, speaks to us eloquently. Composed by Ralph Dutton himself, the inscription reads: 'The last of his line'.

Lydia Greeves
1987

Introduction

The purpose of an introduction is to give the reader a preliminary idea of the scope and intention of the pages which follow, and also perhaps to provide an opportunity for the author to include a few words of becoming apologia for the shortcomings of his work. In any case it is designed to be read first; but in almost all cases, I would suppose, it is in fact written last. Few authors know when they set out on the long and often arduous journey of writing a book precisely how it will develop even when the general objective is clear. Thus the introduction must await events, and be adapted as far as possible to them. In my experience, at any rate, this has always been the sequence, and this little history is no exception.

For a number of years I have had it in mind to assemble such facts as I could gather together about the village of Hinton Ampner, and particularly about the various manor houses which have succeeded each other in it. It is not that it is a place of any importance, one which has had famous inhabitants or can boast outstanding beauty of landscape or architecture, but it represents simply one of the little pieces of the jigsaw which go to make up the full picture of the English countryside. And at the present time when the aspect of England is changing with such alarming speed, there may be some virtue in someone who knows one small area very intimately setting down on paper not only a description of the village as it now is but also some account of the principal house and its inhabitants during the past few centuries.

Hampshire seems at present to be a particularly vulnerable county. The wide area of chalk land which takes up about one-third of the central part of the county is still largely unspoiled, but it lies between the fast expanding town of Basingstoke in the north and the now almost united towns of Southampton and Portsmouth in the south. How long, one wonders, will this pastoral area escape being crushed and swallowed by these menacing jaws which are gradually engulfing the countryside beyond the chalk hills. For how long will little villages like Hinton Ampner and its neighbours survive amongst the undulations of the wide arable fields and the deep sheltering woodlands. For it is in the midst of this area that Hinton lies, 8 miles due east of Winchester, and so almost centrally placed in the chalk country.

Perhaps in describing the rural charms of this area one resembles William Curtis, a famous son of Hampshire, who in the years following 1777 detailed in his *Flora Londinensis* the many wild flowers he found in the fields of Battersea and Bermondsey which were soon to disappear beneath bricks and mortar, and who thus left a botanical record of importance and interest. The resemblance to the present account, I should add, lies not in the importance of the subject, but merely in the description of a possibly passing condition.

My original intention was to detail in historical order such sparse facts as I could accumulate about the inhabitants of the manor house, about the long sequence of squires who lived there since the end of the sixteenth century. There was no uncertainty about their names and about the major dates in their lives of baptism, marriage and death for the Parish Registers dating from 1561 are complete and in good condition, and these could be supplemented by inscriptions on monuments in Hinton church and by names and details mentioned in wills.

I had proposed, however, to avoid the first person singular so far as possible, but as I advanced it seemed to me that the later history of the alterations to the house and to the surroundings might have some general interest, and there is no one except myself who is in a position to describe these developments. Fairly recent happenings soon fade into the mists of the past and insignificant though they are, they may be worth recording. If my predecessors at Hinton had held this view, their notes might now be of absorbing interest. Thus the later chapters become slightly autobiographical, but only in so far as the house is intimately concerned.

Even so the subject remains an exceedingly small one—a mini-subject—but to an author there is one advantage in this: the anxiety lest some other writer, and one of greater ability, is engaged on a work on the same subject, does not exist. No one else, I feel convinced, is compiling a history of Hinton Ampner. This little community which still consists of the traditional group of parish church, Manor House and cluster of cottages, with the addition of a Rectory and a farmhouse or two, remains anonymously buried in the countryside.

The subject matter in the following pages can be divided under three general headings: firstly the village and the countryside in which it lies, with some history of the occupants of the Tudor Manor House; then the various architectural transformations which the house has undergone since the end of the eighteenth century; and finally a description of the development of the garden and the planting of the park. I should probably be optimistic to suppose that any reader would be interested in all three aspects of the place, so it is not unlikely that this little book will fall, not between two but, between three stools—an uncomfortable tumble indeed. However, I must hope that since all three subjects are aspects of the same place this may more or less unite them into a single theme.

A few years ago I noticed a leading article in *The Times* which was headed 'Growing Interest in Local History'. This, at first glance, I thought would be an encouragement to put together such bits and pieces as I could collect about Hinton Ampner. But I was mistaken, for on reading further I found the following chastening passage about amateur local histories:

'Usually compiled by squires, parsons, lawyers, or aldermen, these works of local piety too often reflect their authors' somewhat claustrophobic preoccupation with manorial history, ecclesiology, and municipal institutions; or else they consist of a miscellany of unrelated facts strung together in whatever order struck the compiler's eclectic fancy.'

Here once again, I fear, is a squire compiling what purports to be a little local history, and treating the subject in a closely circumscribed manner, instead of surveying the parish in a broad sweep. It is my belief, however, that there is little in the early history of the village to provide anything which would be of interest except to archaeologists. However, so as not entirely to neglect the subject, I will mention the following few details.

Like the greater part of the ancient Kingdom of Wessex, the parish is an area which has clearly been inhabited beyond all

history, for there are several barrows in the near neighbourhood
of the village. On the slope of the hill across the valley to the north
of the village is a long barrow of considerable size. At one time
there was a tradition that this large mound was raised over the
corpses of the soldiers killed at the Battle of Cheriton in 1644. But
I think this idea is now exploded, and it is accepted that it must
date from the New Stone Age, 2,000 years or so B.C. There are also
a number of round barrows, though some which were in arable
fields have now disappeared through constant ploughing. These
presumably belong to the Bronze Age which ended about 500
B.C. These bare details are all I can offer, I fear, in the way of
pre-history. Passing, then, to A.D., there may well have been a
Roman settlement here, for some years ago a few pieces of pottery
were found when digging took place on the summit of the ridge
to the west of the house. Extensive excavations might produce
something of interest, but there is no definite clue as to what exact
location would be the most promising.

From this point one takes a jump forward of about a thousand
years to the mention of Hinton in the Domesday Survey of 1086.
The following, in clarified language, is the entry:

> 'The Bishop himself (of Winchester) holds Hentune. It was always
> the Minister's. There are 8 hides. In King Edward's time as now it
> paid gold for 5 hides. There is land for 8 ploughs. In the demesne are
> 3 ploughs, and there are 15 villeins and 14 borders with 5 ploughs.
> There are 6 serfs and 8 acres of meadow. There is woodland worth
> 10 swine. There is a church worth 40 shillings but it pays 50 shillings.
> In King Edward's time as now it is worth 8 pounds. When received
> it was worth 100 shillings.'

Hides, which appear in the entry, were small-holdings farmed by
free men, men who had risen above the status of serfdom, while
the villeins were also free men, but cultivated their holdings at the
will of the lord and had various duties to perform in return, and
so were slightly lower in the social scale than the holders of hides.

From here, that is to say from the date of the Survey, this
squire's amateurish history goes forward for another 500 years
until the Stewkeley family make their appearance in the Manor
House, and so far as I know there was nothing particular during
those five centuries of the mediaeval period to record.

It might be supposed that since there has been a continuity of tenure since the end of the sixteenth century that there would be in existence a mass of documents and letters throwing light on the life at Hinton during the seventeenth and eighteenth centuries, but unfortunately almost nothing has survived, so that the Stewkeleys and their successors the Stawells remain rather shadowy characters. I conclude that early in the nineteenth century, when the house was emptied of furniture and let, all papers which must have accumulated over the previous two centuries were destroyed. It is more than possible that my great-grandfather, John Dutton, who came from a staid and level-headed family, thought it prudent to destroy the evidence of the rather raffish lives of his wife's ancestors who had lived at Hinton. However that may be, I have found only one Stewkeley letter of the remotest interest, and this I quote in the following pages.

There are only two incidents in the history of Hinton Ampner which rise above the normal and uneventful story of an old manor house. The first of these is the Battle of Cheriton of 1644 during which it found itself in uncomfortable proximity to the fighting; and the second is the ghost story of the following century. The latter has been recounted in a number of books on the subject of supernatural manifestations, but I have repeated it in the following pages with such additional details as have been handed down to me.

The tenure of the Hinton Ampner estate was a curious one. From the time that Sir Thomas Stewkeley first took a lease of the Manor, possibly at the time of his marriage in 1597, until 1863 the estate remained copyhold, the owner paying a small fine to the Dean and Chapter of Winchester who remained the ground landlords. In a legal opinion given in 1834 on some point to do with the property I found the following preamble:

> 'Tenure of the Copyhold Estates is of inheritance with ancient and accustomed fines at sums certain and Heriots due on the Death of the tenants, or alienation.'

At intervals during the seventeenth and eighteenth centuries documents were drawn up referring to various parts of the property and always citing the descent from Sir Thomas Stewkeley. It seems that all the owners of the copyhold treated the place as entirely their own property, Sir Hugh Stewkeley having his baronetcy created of Hinton Ampner, and the last Lord Stawell demolishing the Manor House and building another. But during all this time the Dean and Chapter remained the Lords of the Manor, and it was not until 1863 that my grandfather enfranchised the property, thus leaving only the advowson of the living in the hands of the Dean and Chapter.

There is one final note I would like to add to this introduction, and it is this. Although there are obvious advantages in writing about a place one knows very intimately, there is also one disadvantage: one is inclined to lose one's critical faculty. Books of travel and chatty guide books are often most successful when written by authors who do not know the country too well. They can convey an impression which is very vivid to a reader, since they see everything with a fresh eye, and can seize on points which are notable to them and so are interesting to record.

This is clearly not my position with Hinton: upwards of 70 years have blurred any critical vision, although the house and its surroundings have changed vastly since I came into the world. And with these changes there is also a slight difficulty. Since they are my own work, should I praise them when they seem to have been successful? Self-praise is not becoming, and in any case it may seem to many misplaced. However, it is a chance one must take, for descriptions in which the writer does not venture an opinion make dull reading.

The Parish and the Church

CRISIS

One of the minor social changes which has taken place during my lifetime is the method of announcing births in the public press. Nowadays the parents are familiarly mentioned by their Christian names, there then may follow the names of children with which the couple have already been blessed, and to which the new born is to form an agreeable addition, and finally there may appear the Christian names of the new infant which would seem to have been settled at top speed. A short pedigree in fact.

The announcement of my arrival as printed on the outside page of *The Times*, and no doubt of *The Morning Post* as well, was a more reserved affair:

> On 25th August 1898 at Hinton Ampner House, Hampshire Mrs. Henry Dutton, of a son.

Thus there was no more than an indirect reference to my father, and no indelicate recognition that a union of the sexes had produced this result. Perhaps feeling slighted, my father omitted to register the birth of his son and heir, which had occurred after 10 years of marriage and subsequent to the births of two daughters, for a number of weeks, and when he eventually did so, made a mistake in the month, so that my birth certificate assures me that I appeared in this world on the 25th September, and thus my birthday remains in the official records of Somerset House.

I mention these unimportant details to indicate to the reader the mature age of the author, and also to show the long connection I have had with the village, or rather the principal house in it, to which this little book is devoted. Still to live in the place where one was born very many years ago, at least ensures that one knows a small area of the earth's surface tolerably well, and I hope excuses writing about a place which is of minimal historical importance.

The house into which my introduction was announced in such dignified terms was a mid-Victorian building of exceptional hideousness. It was distinctly large, even by the standards of those spacious days, and deserved, I think, to be called a 'mansion'. If this epithet is one of praise, it is probably the only kind word which could have been found for the house. But in fact it had one good feature which could not have been apparent to an observer: behind the plate-glass windows and barge-boarded gables there still stood, engulfed in the flood of Victorian Tudor, the fabric of a simple late Georgian building. This unexpected survival of eighteenth-century decorum was to be of great value to me 37 years after my birth.

The Georgian building was by no means the first on the site. It had been built in 1793 when a Tudor house, standing 60 yards to the north, had been demolished. And the Tudor manor had replaced a very dimly recorded mediaeval building which was said to have been destroyed by fire early in the sixteenth century. Thus it can be fairly said that the site has been occupied domestically for five centuries, and possibly much longer. But before looking—in so far as sparse records will allow—at the various houses which have arisen here during these centuries, it may be as well to provide some description of the general situation, and this may give an indication why the site has remained in domestic occupation although the house standing there has been destroyed or demolished five times in five centuries.

There are, I think, more than fifteen villages named Hinton scattered about England, each distinguished by an additional name as prefix or suffix. The prevalence of the name is not surprising since the meaning is simple: *Tun* is Old English for homestead, and *Hea* means on high ground. There is an alternative definition, however. *Hin* may derive from *Higna*, the complete word thus meaning the Tun or homestead belonging to monks or nuns. As it happens either of these derivations would fit the Hinton of this book equally well, for it is not only on a hill, but it also belonged for centuries to the Priory of St. Swithun at Winchester. It is this connection which provided the suffix of *Ampner*, for this is a corruption of the word *Almoner*, the manor having been the particular appurtenance of the Almoner of the Priory.

In some old deeds instead of the suffix Almoner or Ampner, it was simply called Prior's Hinton, but in the end the first nomenclature won the day.

Now having more or less settled the origin of the name of the parish, one may glance at its physical characteristics. It covers a fairly large area, 2,378 acres to be exact, but it has always been sparsely populated, and civilly it has long been amalgamated with the adjacent parish of Bramdean. Ecclesiastically it retains its individuality, and the scattered group of cottages lying on the east side of the deep road which rises from the main Winchester to Peterfield highway, although in appearance no more than a hamlet, qualifies technically as a village since it boasts a parish church, to which the road leads. The parish also, surprisingly enough, contains two public houses, the *Jolly Farmer* on its extreme western boundary and apparently in Cheriton, and the *Fox* a mile away to the east amongst the cottages of Bramdean but within the confines of the parish of Hinton Ampner. Two pubs and a church give this modest parish a certain status even if the clientele of the former is principally drawn from motorists on the high road and the sparse congregation at the latter is slightly strengthened by worshippers from the village of Bramdean.

The village, such as it is, lies on the north slope of a long ridge, with the church and Hinton Ampner House on its summit. To the east the ridge stretches away for 8 or 9 miles till it ends abruptly above the village of Langrish, but to the west the grounds begin to fall gently to a valley within a few hundred yards of church and house, so that both stand on a mild promontory from which slopes descend to the north and south, and a little more distantly to the west. At the base of the west end of the promontory lies the official source of the River Itchen—in a willow-filled dell on the east side of the lane to the village of Kilmeston. In the valley many springs make their contribution to the small trickle which emerges from the 'official source', which, it must be owned, in a dry season hardly deserves its title, although in a wet season it projects a fine clear stream beneath the bridge carrying the Kilmeston lane.

During my lifetime the village—for such we will call it—has altered remarkably little. A few new cottages have been built, mostly taking the place of those that were substandard, but there are still a number of highly picturesque buildings of half timber and thatch which may well have stood here since the seventeenth century or before. The majority of these group near the point where the steep road I have already mentioned leaves the highway, and it is this road which gives, I think, a pleasant feeling of antiquity to the place. It rises in a rather wide gentle curve up the hill and for the greater part of its length lies deep below the level of the adjacent land, worn down by centuries of wheeled carts and rainwater. Along the top of the steep banks grow tall trees, many of them ancient oaks, which increase both the sense of depth and age.

The road mounts past the former Rectory, now renamed Hinton Ampner Place, which is a reminder of the spacious days of the country parson. The trim brick front, built during the reign of the first King George, rises on the east side, and the windows look out over the park of Hinton Ampner House which covers the slope to the west. The original steep bank is here converted into a terrace in front of the house, bounded by a wall, and on to which a flight of steps leads through a central gateway.

By good fortune the date of the building of the house is known, for the Rector-builder was not backward in recording his achievements. On the first page of the Parish Registers, opposite the extremely neat entries of 1561, he wrote in a flourishing eighteenth-century hand, with a considerable spluttering of ink from his quill pen, an account of what he had done:

> Kenwick Puleston, sometime Fellow of Jesus College, Oxon, and Batchelor of Divinity, Vicar of Corse-Lawn near Glocester, and Rector of this Parish of Hinton (Amner). He re-built ye greater part of ye Parlour new from ye foundations to ye Ridge of ye Roof in June about midsummer in this year of our Lord 1717.
>
> Besides ye new part of ye Parlour of ye Parsonage House. He repaired ye east side of ye old house partly with brick building intirely new and partly with filling up pannels with bricks and bonded well; ye same he did, as it were all new, on ye south side of ye long Gallery—study. Ye same he did on ye east side of ye old back building. And in ye year of Or. Lord God 1712 he new laid ye Roof of ye Kitchen all ye north side with extraordinary good Laths and Tiles.

It is not very easy to follow Mr. Puleston's rebuilding programme for the house now appears to be all of a piece, except for an addition on the north side which was made in the 1880s, but which followed the style of the existing building, and is innocuous.

Returning to the road, Hinton Hill, as it is known, bears to the east as it nears the top of the rise and leads away past Manor Farm and, skirting the park, forms a wide loop southward till it reaches the village of Kilmeston. At the point where it bears east, a private road bordered by clipped box and holly bushes leads straight on through iron gates set between tall stone piers into the garden of Hinton Ampner House, passing close beside the wall of the churchyard within which stands the church. Across a wide extent of lawn, on which rise some large specimens of hardwood trees, lies the house, with a gently sloping forecourt in front of it, while beyond it can be glimpsed the landscape which extends away to the south.

To those interested in geology, Hinton Hill provides more than an agreeable approach to church and house, for in the steep banks can be seen the two materials which form the subsoil for the whole of this part of the county—chalk and clay. Basically this area is a chalk country, but although in places it comes to within a few inches of the surface, there are many others where it is overlain by a deep covering of stiff clay, and it is this clay which forms a cap along much of the Hinton Ampner ridge. Here and there are rare pockets of a good and nearly lime-free loam, rewarding to gardeners, while in the valleys on either side of the ridge are stretches of gravel beds, the disused pits along the north valley showing that gravel digging was here once actively undertaken. This may well have been at the time when the Winchester/ Petersfield road was being improved, and it was natural to use the material which lay so conveniently at hand. It is through the clay which covers the north slope of the ridge that rainwater rushing down to the valley, and aided by the wheels of past centuries, has carved the deep road.

This simplified description of the geology of the area is adequate to account for the landscape which lies above it. It cannot boast grand scenery: there is little of the luxuriance of woodland and hedgerow timber to be found in Sussex, or the dramatic contrast of massive open downs interspersed with deep leafy valleys as in Wiltshire. The central chalk area of Hampshire is indeed a compromise between the two. Several long chalk ridges rising in places to over 700 feet run east and west across this part of the country, and between them lies a complexity of undulations so that a level area of any size is rare. So rare indeed are these

areas, that several villages in the locality find it difficult to dis-
cover a site suitable for a cricket field. That at Hinton, for example, which is in the park to the west of the house and has
served this purpose for many decades, has a distinct tilt to the
north and so provides at least an initial advantage to the home
team which knows the peculiarities of the ground.

If the landscape lacks grandeur, it at least has a gentle beauty
with its low hills covered with spacious arable fields, interspersed
with areas of dark woodland which usually indicate a pocket of
clay soil. It is a landscape which depends for its beauty on its
trees: of hedgerow timber there is not very much but of natural
woodland there is a good area, while former landowners have
crowned the chalk ridges in their possession with plantations of
beech trees, thus agreeably breaking their rather austere outlines.
It is a landscape which changes its colouring throughout the year
with the growth of the crops, for there is much arable land. The
dark umber of plough turns miraculously to jade green as the
young corn begins to shoot; the green to a pale yellow, and the
yellow to gold as the crop ripens, and so back after harvest to
yellow with the stubble until the ground is turned once more by
the plough. This rotation is a commonplace, constantly described,
and yet the fascination of the changing scene never fails to exercise
its charm.

The house stands at the fairly modest elevation of 360 feet, but
since the high road in the valley is 100 feet lower, the contrast
gives an increased sense of altitude. From the house there is a wide
view southward over the placid landscape, with barely a building
in sight. In the middle distance lies the village of Kilmeston, but
it is completely concealed by trees and the folds of the ground.
Beyond these trees the ground rises to the long down-like ridge
of the Millbarrow hills which, under various names, stretch from
the valley of the Meon in the east to the valley of the Itchen in the
west. Away to the east, rising above woodlands and beyond the
Meon valley, can be seen the bold outline of Old Winchester Hill,
one of the highest downs in the county. How it came by this name
is unknown, for as the crow flies, it is 12 miles or more from the
City of Winchester, which, with its Roman or pre-Roman origins,
is no modern foundation.

On the west the country undulates in gentle contours away to
Cheesefoot Head, the last high point of the ridge before it drops

gradually to the Itchen valley and to Winchester. No landscape could be more serene and more completely rural, and yet the two great Hampshire ports, Southampton and Portsmouth, lie at no very great distance beyond the Millbarrow hills, respectively about 18 and 25 miles from Hinton. At night, when the cloud formation is favourable, the reflection of their lights shines in the sky, a reminder of the busy world beyond the dark horizon.

It must, I think, have been this peaceful prospect which first led to the building of a house at Hinton, and which persuaded a succession of owners not to abandon the site in spite of the various reverses which occurred. It was certainly the prime influence in my own building operations.

It was across this landscape that William Cobbett passed during the month of November 1822, travelling from the market town of Alresford to the village of Exton in the Meon valley, a journey of 10 miles or so which he described in *Rural Rides*. His route lay by Cheriton, Beauworth, Kilmeston, then over the Millbarrow ridge, and so down into the river valley. Hinton fortunately lay a mile or so off his path to the north, or it might have earned a few searing animadversions on absentee landlords. However, his general description of the area and the gloomy picture he paints of the condition of farming is interesting:

> The whole country that I have crossed is loam and flints upon a bottom of chalk. . . . These counties are purely agricultural; they have suffered most cruelly from the accursed Pitt-system. Their hilliness, bleakness, roughness of roads, render them unpleasant to the luxurious, effeminate, tax-eating, crew who never come near them, and who have pared them down to the very bone. . . . The villages are all in a state of *decay*, the farm buildings dropping down, bit by bit.

Pitt by that time had been dead for 16 years, but in Cobbett's view the damage done by his policy was still alive and the decay of the countryside was due to the taxes he had imposed. He prophesied that within 40 years the whole farming community would be ruined. In the event the reverse occurred, and the 1860s were a period of great prosperity both for farmers and landlords.

When farming was once again in the doldrums in the years between the wars it was assumed that from chalk land a farmer could barely scratch a livelihood, just as it was by many supposed that those living on chalk might as well abandon all effort to have

a decent garden. In both cases this defeatism has now very defi-
nitely changed, and with new methods these chalk and clay lands
can vie with the best corn-growing areas in the country; while for
gardeners there is no longer any cause for despair, and they can
take heart from the achievements of Sir Edward Stern in his
majestic chalkpit near Worthing, and those of Mr. Lewis Palmer
on a smaller scale at Headbourne Worthy, near Winchester.

There are two unmistakable signs that in past centuries this was
not prosperous farming land—there are almost no great and
famous country houses within the area, and with very few exceptions the parish churches are modest in scale. The few outstanding
houses in Hampshire lie near its boundaries and away from the
chalk country: Bramshill, The Vyne, Stratfield Saye, Hackwood
in the extreme north, Braemare to the west. The Grange near
Alresford is perhaps an exception, but the money which transformed in the early nineteenth century a moderate-sized house
into a mansion of magnificence came from banking and not from
the land.

The old churches in the area bear no comparison with the
splendid parish churches of Norfolk, for example, or those in the
limestone country of Gloucestershire; and those fine churches, of
which there are a few in the county, will with rare exceptions be
found to be away from the chalk subsoil. The average Hampshire
church is a humble building with little claim to interest beyond a
respectable antiquity. A nave without aisles, a small chancel, and
at the west end a low weather-boarded belfry: that was the
general style of church in small parishes, and they were well
suited to the worship of a sparse community. The Church of All
Saints at Hinton Ampner was just such a simple little building
until the passion for improvement which pervaded the nineteenth
century led to its transformation into something more in accord
with the taste of the period.

The site of the church is impressive standing as it does on the
very crest of the ridge. When the first church was raised here in
pre-Conquest times the site must have been quite dramatic, and
the little church would have been visible to those working in the
fields for a long way round. Now, surrounded by trees, it is not
visible until one is in its close proximity at the summit of the hill.
It stands comfortably within its well-kept churchyard, now no
longer in use; and is only separated from the garden of Hinton

Ampner House by a wall on the south side and a holly hedge on the west.

The parish registers date back to the year 1561 and form a useful and accurate record of the baptisms, marriages and deaths of the inhabitants of the parish. Only rarely, unfortunately, did an incumbent follow the example of the Rev. Kenrick Puleston and break away from the simple statement of names and dates and insert some scrap of information about the parish or the church.

It is surprising how the population of the parish must have decreased in four centuries. In 1563, for example, which admittedly was rather a bumper year, there were six christenings, three marriages and seven burials. Only in one case, that of Christian Woods, did the infant who was baptized hurry out of this world three days later. In 1963 there was only one of each of the first two, and two of the third; and this also was something of a bumper year. No doubt families were much larger in the sixteenth century, but they must also have lived in infinitely more crowded conditions than now, for there is no indication that the number of cottages in the village was ever greater than today. In fact my grandfather built ten cottages, and I have added five but nevertheless the total of the population would appear to have decreased.

About the alterations to the structure of the church the parish registers remain tantalizingly mute; except for one entry which I will shortly mention. A photograph taken I think soon after 1860 by my grandmother, who was an early and keen photographer, shows the west end of the church with the porch and wooden belfry. From this it would appear that a good deal had survived from the Saxon building but that various windows, purely domestic in style, had been inserted in Tudor times to supplement the dim daylight that filtered through the narrow lancets, and that the porch had been added at the same period.

The chancel, which does not appear in the photograph, had already undergone two transformations. Perhaps the original church had none. If so this lack was remedied in the thirteenth century when a spacious and well-built chancel was erected with a vault beneath it. It contained a rather elaborate two-storied double piscina, a sedilia, a squint and a small north doorway. All these features still survive but were so thoroughly rechiselled at the next alteration in the early nineteenth century that they now bear a singularly spurious air. The exact date of this work is unknown, but it must have been before 1822, the date which appears at the base of the two long east windows which are filled with glass of exceptional crudity.

On the whole, however, this early nineteenth-century work was rather well carried out. The squared flintwork with which the exterior is faced presumably dates from this period, and is impressive if one considers the amount of time and work entailed in cutting flints to the size of small bricks, varying in length, but all of an almost uniform 3 inches in depth so that they can be set in even lines, and form a fairly smooth general surface.

The other agreeable feature of the chancel is the wooden roof of the interior. It is a tradition that it is made from timber supplied by the last Lord Stawell, and brought from his estate in the West Indies. If there is any truth in this, the wood must be some sort of Caribbean cedar. But as with many traditions the story seems unlikely as the woodwork would appear to date from much earlier than the beginning of the nineteenth century. It may have been one of Mr. Puleston's improvements, for once again, modestly blowing his own trumpet, he wrote in the Register:

> In ye year 1713 new Roofed ye Chancel all over, with new laths and Tiles extraordinary strong and good as ever were laid on a church.

The design would seem to be a more likely product of the reign of George I than George IV, and indeed with its boldly moulded ribs between sunken panels it could date from the latter part of the previous century. But fashion changed slowly in country districts, and 1713 would seem a quite probable date.

There are also in the chancel two charming monuments to children of the Stewkeley family. The earlier, which is quite small, is to Thomas, who was born on the 10th October 1601 and died ten days later. The body of the infant is portrayed lying on a sarcophagus wrapped in a crimson shroud edged with gold and beneath an arch intended, no doubt, to represent a vault. On either side decorated pilasters support a cornice, and are an agreeable early essay in Renaissance design.

The other is to another Thomas of the following generation who died 30th March 1638 aged three years. It is far more elaborate, and in its uncontrolled flamboyance is more typical of a rather earlier age. Although not large in scale it manages to incorporate in its composition not only a recumbent figure of the child, but also an angel flying amongst clouds sounding the Last Trump, in company with the heads of a number of winged putti, a flaming heart, a celestial crown supported by angels, a sun, moon and stars. The whole tumult of heavenly paraphernalia is framed in Corinthian pillars supporting a pediment and decorated with a lavish display of heraldry. A third monument to the last male Stewkeley, Sir Hugh, who died in 1719, shows admirable restraint both in design and colouring.

There are several seventeenth-century brasses to members of the Stewkeley family, one handsomely heraldic to the first Sir Hugh who died in 1642, while a simple plate embellished with a verse more outstanding for ingenuity than poetic feeling commemorates the death of Elizabeth, daughter of the 2nd Sir Hugh at the age of 37 weeks in 1667:

> *Reader within this little vault lies pent*
> *The ashes of a female innocent,*
> *Whose early whiter soule as yet hath not*
> *From the defileing world contracted spott.*
> *The day she lived, she dyed, yet having spent*
> *some few moneths so to Abram's bossome went,*
> *Where now her happy soule enjoys that Blisse*
> *Which unto little infants promised is:*
> *Now who this harmless St. was wouldst thou know,*
> *Look down and read th' inscription here below.*

At a period when infant mortality was so usual it seems strange that these babies should have been so carefully, indeed expensively, commemorated.

These monuments fortunately survived my grandfather's enthusiasm for destroying memorials from the past, but many others he removed and put in the vault when he rebuilt the nave in the 1870s. At the same time as the nave was rebuilt the pews in the chancel were replaced with the solid pitch pine which seems to have found such grace in nineteenth-century eyes, while the floor was raised and laid with many-coloured Doulton tiles, and massive brass altar rails (now removed) guarded the Sanctuary. The builders of the last century were convinced they could improve by adding, nowadays we believe we can improve by taking away: it is difficult to foresee what the next movement will be.

The chancel on the whole escaped lightly: the ancient nave on the other hand, which had stood for centuries, was demolished to the foundations. This was due to the combined enthusiasm of my grandfather and the Rector. When the former had completed the rebuilding of his house, which lay less than 100 yards away across the laurel bushes, the Rector had said to him: 'Now that you have rebuilt your own house, won't you rebuild the house of God?' Whether it was due to his piety or to his sadly undiscriminating passion for building it is impossible to say, but the appeal fell on fertile ground, and within a year or two a solid and severe flint structure had replaced the old nave in which villagers, farmers and squires—some of the last in distinct need of spiritual uplift— had gathered over centuries for their weekly devotions.

Given my grandfather's complete lack of taste, the result might well have been worse, and it would seem that he must have been guided by a sensible architect or a capable builder. A church which he erected on his property at Kingsley near Alton was considerably less innocuous. A few remnants from the pre-Conquest building were incorporated—shafts of long and short stonework were re-used amongst the flintwork on both the north and south sides, and the south doorway with its semicircular arch and stout stone reveals was re-erected as an entrance to the new vestry on the north side. The date of the robust oak door which fills the doorway is known, for on it is carved 'Nicholas Lacey gave this Door February 1643'. The donor was buried at Hinton in the same month, so no doubt he left a bequest for a new outer door for the church, the position where this was until the rebuilding.

In addition to the Stewkeleys there are three families whose names constantly appear in the Registers: Lacey, Earwacker and Camis. The first two were farmers, and are sometimes so designated, but the last, who were extremely prolific, seem to have been smallholders or farm labourers. The Laceys must have lived at Manor Farm, and the Earwackers—a strange name, not unusual in Hampshire—were certainly at the adjacent farm for it bore their name until this century when it came to be called by the simpler name of Godwin's Farm after a subsequent tenant. The two first names disappear from the Registers about 1820, but the Camises do not vanish till 1862, by which time they must have lived at least three centuries in the parish, but without raising their status in the world for in the last entry Robert Camis is described as 'Labourer'.

The bell tower at the west end is topped by a wooden structure which is clearly intended to emulate the belfry which it replaced, but, owing to the Victorian partiality for improving on original designs, it has a Swiss rather than a Hampshire air.

The bells survived the rebuilding, and all three are dated, two 1603 and the third 1719. The two first, which are inscribed 'Serv God' and 'Fere God', bear also the initials of the caster, J. W. for John Wallis of the Salisbury Bell Foundry. The third, the tenor bell, has the following words on it: 'My hope in God is'. This was a motto often used by John Higden, so it seems likely to be his work, and is probably a mediaeval bell recast. All three bells have an agreeable tone.

Almost as sad as the loss of the original nave is the loss of the monuments, of which I believe there were many. The entrance to the vault, into which they were thrust, was so carefully sealed that I have no clue to its whereabouts and I have so far been unable to examine them, or the coffins of the generations of owners, with their spouses and children which lie there. A number of names and dates were gathered on to a mutilated tablet which is set above the font at the west end, while below it are two finely carved features from other monuments.

The walls of the nave are not, however, absolutely bare, for in 1952 I transported here two interesting monuments from the church of St. Mary at Laverstoke near Whitchurch. By chance I read in the county weekly, the *Hampshire Chronicle*, an account of the last service held in that little church before its demolition. Many years earlier I had visited the church and seen the monument to the first wife of the last Sir Hugh Stewkeley, who had died in 1679. She was the heiress of the Laverstoke estate and had been buried there, rather than at Hinton with the other members of her husband's family. The rather equivocal lines on the monument, which I will quote later when we look at the Stewkeley family, might indicate that the bonds between her and Sir Hugh were not of the closest.

I learnt from the incumbent of Laverstoke that as no one wished to take the monument to Lady Stewkeley, it had been decided to dismantle it and seal it up in the vault, just as my grandfather had done at Hinton in unenlightened Victorian times. The Rector's search for a home for the monument cannot have been very exhaustive since it was shown on the inscription that the lady was the wife of Sir Hugh Stewkeley of Hinton Ampner.

I at once agreed to take the monument and also one to her parents which was likewise doomed to oblivion, and to re-erect them at Hinton, and there they now are on the south wall of the nave. The disappearance of Lady Stewkeley's monument would have been unfortunate for it is of unusual design, and according to the late Rupert Gunnis is almost certainly the work of that highly individual sculptor, John Bushnell. It consists of a bust of Katherine Stewkeley set in a niche draped with marble curtains and flanked by a pair of marble urns; below is the inscription carved on the leaves of an open book. For a monument of moderate size it achieves a considerable sense of the dramatic. The monument to Katherine's parents which dates from 1672 is conventional, and has of course no real connection with Hinton, but the workmanship is good. On the north wall is a monument designed by Trenwith Wills, which I erected to my parents. In the pediment are the Dutton arms quartered with those of the families from whom my father was descended and who had in turn owned the Hinton estate—Stewkeley, Stawell and Legge. At the base of the tablet a space awaits the insertion of my name and dates.

When I was very young the church was invariably well filled for Matins on Sunday mornings. We as a family occupied a pew and a half, the Rector's family did likewise. There were seldom any other gentry, since indeed there were hardly any others in the parish, but the gardeners and their wives, and the farm labourers with their families, made up a congregation of respectable size. There were also three benches at the back of the church given up to the children from the village school who sat under the severe eye of the school mistress. In front of the children the maids and men-servants from the house filled a couple of benches. The upper maids wore toques and the underlings small black bonnets. I remember how this custom broke down. During the Four Years War, in 1915 I think, when the men-servants had joined the army, a parlour-maid was engaged, a tall, handsome young woman. On the first Sunday morning after her arrival she came to church in large hat. In a HAT, if you please! Consternation. But after some anxious discussion it was decided in view of the general situation—

the German's second great struggle for Ypres and the Channel Ports had just begun, and poison gas had been loosed for the first time on to the British troops—to let it pass. But the rot was setting in and traditions were crumbling: soon bonnets and toques disappeared from the back of the church and hats took their place.

I have perhaps said too much about this unimportant church, which at least to a superficial glance is little more than a commonplace nineteenth-century building, and we will now leave it and cross the narrow strip of churchyard to the iron gate, which originally guarded the entrance to the porch, and so pass into the garden of the house which is the hero—or heroine—of these pages.

The Tudor Manor House

At the start a few words should be said about the early history of Hinton Ampner, but they will indeed be few for there is little to be said. There were no famous names connected with it in mediaeval times, no exciting events to record, no seizures by the Crown, no handing out as a reward to a deserving subject. Its history seems to have been completely uneventful. It was already in the possession of the Bishop of Winchester at the time of the Domesday Survey (1086), and it appears to have remained quietly attached to the Priory of St. Swithun at Winchester for the following four and a half centuries.

The Dissolution of the Monasteries in 1535 had no dramatic repercussions for the Manor. It simply passed into the possession of the Dean and Chapter of Winchester Cathedral and continued its uneventful existence. During the régime of the Priory there was apparently a small house standing close to the west end of the church, and this is thought to have been burnt down about the time of the Dissolution. This is no more than a vague tradition: there is no exact record of the occurrence, and equally nothing to indicate its position, but the fact that the next building erected arose on a site so unusual for a Tudor manor house suggests that it may have replaced the previous manor. In any case the re-building must have been undertaken soon after the estate came into the possession of the Dean and Chapter of Winchester.

During the Tudor period there were generally two prime considerations when choosing a site for a house—shelter and a water supply. Thus houses were usually situated in a valley where hills and trees protected the building from the winds, and no more than a shallow well would provide an adequate supply of water. There must then have been some good reason for these sixteenth-century builders to erect a house on the very summit of the ridge where it would be fully exposed to every wind, and where it would appear to have been a difficult task to sink a well sufficiently deep to provide water. It is possible that the well was already in existence, and that this had been found to tap an underground spring at no very great depth. This fact and the proximity of the church may have outweighed fears about exposure to the elements. The well, it may be added, still exists and, now considerably deepened, provides the house with fresh, pure water very different from the flat chemically treated supply which comes from the mains.

The house then built was to survive for more than two centuries, but no picture, no drawing of it, apparently exists. No one seems to have thought of perpetuating its appearance before its demolition in 1793. There is, however, one clue to its appearance: a plan, a very elementary plan. This is included amongst the papers of Admiral Lord St. Vincent, at the British Museum (for reasons which will appear later) and shows at least the outline of the house and also the position of some of the rooms. This, with some knowledge of the general trend of vernacular domestic architecture of the period, makes it possible to build up a picture of this vanished house.

It was in the familiar form of an E with slightly projecting end wings and a porch rather to the west of centre, facing almost due south; the north front was apparently flat. There were two main floors with attic rooms for the servants in the roof, and it was clearly of ample size. There was a great hall, two parlours and 21 bedchambers, in addition to kitchens, bakery, larders and service rooms, as well as a brewhouse and a malthouse, which were necessary in order to make a country house largely self-supporting. Near the house was a hop-garden which with the barley from the estate presumably provided the raw materials to justify the two latter buildings. But hops, it seems, must have changed in character if they consented to grow in this unsuitable, limey soil.

Enlightening particulars of the house are provided by a survey made in 1649, when the Manor and estate were seized by Parliament and put up for sale. The original manuscript still exists in the Cathedral Library at Winchester. The preamble to the particulars is as follows:

A Survey of the Manno^r of Hinton Ampner ... in the month of August 1649 by virtue of a Commission to us granted upon an Act of the Commons of England assembled in Parliament for the abolishing of Deans, Dean and Chapters, Canons, Prebends and other officers and Tythe of and belonging to any Cathedral or Collegiate Church or Chappell within England and Wales.

There then follows in addition to the details already given a list of the following outbuildings:

A rush house, a mill house, a bake house, a nursery, a foulding house, a well house, a drove house, a granary and stable, all covered with tyle, built the greatest part with brick and stone, the rest of the dwelling house with Timber and Flemish wall, also a Malthouse, three Stables under one roof, two great barns, and several outhouses, all built with timber and covered with thatch, and two gardens, two orchards well planted, a handsome large Court, well walled, a large outyard and a well yard, also a handsome bowling green with a little house thereon.

It was altogether a considerable establishment; but in case these particulars were not adequate to attract a buyer, the survey describes further charms:

The site of the house is very pleasantly situated, a good Ayre, very delightful for hunting and hawking, six miles distant from the City of Winchester, 2 miles from the market town of Alresford and 12 miles from Southampton.

It must be said that Hinton has receded considerably from these three towns during the past three centuries.

The delights of the place successfully attracted a buyer in one Sir John Hippesley who paid the sum of £2,587 17s. 5½d. for the Manor. Nothing further is heard about Sir John, and one supposes he made a bad bargain, for the estate was returned to the Dean and Chapter on the Restoration in 1660, and the Stewkeley family remained in possession of their hereditary copyhold paying the septennial fine.

There is some interest in the description of the house as being built in brick and stone. There is no stone available in the near neighbourhood, and it may perhaps have been brought from Selborne. It would have been used for quoins at the corners of the house, for outlining the gables, and for the surrounds and mullions of the casement windows. The bricks, on the other hand, may have been produced almost on the site, for part of the park is traditionally known as the Brick Field, and in it is a large pit from

which the clay may have been dug and burnt in a kiln there built
for the purpose.

It seems to have been a simple building, very similar to many
other manor houses which were erected during the decades on
either side of 1550 in the vernacular style before the new-fangled
ideas of the Renaissance had begun to percolate into the countryside. The survey mentions that the parlours were 'wainscoted',
so these rooms must have been lined with the small-scale panelling
which was usual at that period. The hall, which was apparently
entered direct from the porch without a screens passage as would
have been the case at a rather earlier date, was only one storey
in height. At least in the plan drawn in the eighteenth century
there were bedrooms over it on the first floor, though it is possible,
of course, that these had been introduced in the seventeenth
century.

A point I have not been able to elucidate is who built the house.
It seems unlikely that the Dean and Chapter would have gone to
the expense of erecting so large a building, and it seems more
probable that they leased the property on a copyhold tenure to
some family on the condition that they replaced the destroyed
building with a new manor house. It would have been this lease
that Thomas Stewkeley took over just before 1600 when the name
of this family first appears in the Church Registers.

This entry is Thomas' marriage to Mrs. Elizabeth Goodwin on
30th June 1597. His younger brother George was also married
at Hinton five years later to Mrs. Elizabeth Drewell. Elizabeth
Goodwin was the daughter and sole heiress of John Goodwin of
Over Winchenden in Buckinghamshire. Her inheritance, however, does not appear to have materialized quite as easily as
Thomas had no doubt hoped, for in 1600 a case was brought in
the 'Queen's Court at Westminster' by Francis Goodwin against
'Thomas Stewkeley Armiger and Elizabeth his wife', claiming
the property covering apparently over 3,000 acres at Upper
Winchenden and Waddesden. This Francis may have been an
uncle or cousin of Elizabeth's: he was certainly not a brother. He
seems to have had a fairly good claim, for the case was settled by
the payment of £2,000 to the Stewkeleys in exchange for the
property.

It remains a mystery, however, why Thomas and Elizabeth
were married at Hinton when neither appears to have had any

previous connection with the place. There are, it is true, various entries in the Registers of Godwins, with every possible variety of spelling, but there seems nothing to connect these with the family from Over (or Upper) Winchenden. It is just possible, however, that it was a member of the Godwin family who built the house.

This Thomas Stewkeley, who was the first of my ancestors to live at Hinton, came from Marsh near Dunster, in Somerset, where his family had been settled for several generations and where they seem to have owned considerable property, some of which their descendants retained until this century. I have the impression that they were hardheaded people, good at business and with a shrewd eye for an heiress.

The very long and detailed will which Thomas' father made in 1587, the year before his death, shows that he had extensive property in Somerset, and also interests in London. He asks that if he should die in the latter place he should be buried in the chancel of St. Sepulchre's 'in the suburbs of the City of London', but if in Somerset then in 'the chancel of the late priory church of Dunster over against my seat or pew'. In the event it was Dunster which received his bones. After a number of small legacies to relations, godsons and household servants 'as long as they do behave themselves honestly and dutifully', he left £100 to Lady Burleigh 'to get the wardship of my heir'. Thomas Stewkeley was then eighteen years old so the wardship would not have been of long duration. But perhaps he thought that Lady Burleigh would see that his wish was fulfilled that 'my son Thomas apply his study in the Common Laws of this Realm of England in the Inner Temple, London'. Until he became an 'utter barrister' the boy was to be given £24 a year for his maintenance, and £30 when he had achieved this status.

On his marriage Thomas' condition was to brighten somewhat for he was to receive all his father's plate, including 'my best bason and ewer parcel gilt, and my great nest of bowls parcel gilt, my best salt with a cover gilt', and much else of the same sort, although a large part of it could be used by his widow 'if she keep herself unmarried'. Under the same condition she receives 'my mansion house at Marsh' with its contents and all the livestock, and lands and tenements in the parishes of Marsh, Carhampton and Dunster, including 'the rectory and parsonage' at the last, 'with all the tithes great or small'.

There then follows a long list of Manors in Somerset and Devon which are to be held in trust for some years and then go to his son Thomas and his heirs male, and, if these fail, then to the second son George. The latter anyhow receives all the lands in Stepney, Whitechapel, Fulham, Ealing and Brentford, in County Middlesex, and then to his heirs male; but if these fail, then back to Thomas. All this, and there is a good deal more in the will, indicates very substantial wealth, nevertheless the three daughters receive no more than £100 apiece, but an additional £566 13s. 4d. if they marry with their mother's approval. Clearly Hugh Stewkeley had no intention of allowing the estate, which he had built up, being dissipated amongst daughters.

Thomas Stewkeley who, as has been said, was married at Hinton, had three surviving sons all of whom were bred to the Law like their father. They were entered at the Middle Temple, the elder two in 1621 and the youngest in 1626, and their legal training must have been useful to them in their careers. Thomas was knighted by James I soon after his accession. It was no doubt one of those honours that the King handed out very freely—and at no cost to himself—to landowners and squires whose influence in the country was an important factor in maintaining the stability of the Crown. Local gentry in hundreds received the accolade, and in return became warmly attached to the royal cause.

Thomas' eldest son Hugh did even better than his father, and in 1627 obtained a baronetcy. This was a more substantial honour and was perhaps awarded by Charles I on the principle inaugurated by his father in return for a *douceur* of between £1,000 and £2,000 which was supposed to go towards the maintenance of the army in Ulster, but was in fact more usually devoted to personal debts. In any case the young man was only 24 years of age when he blossomed into Sir Hugh Stewkeley of Hinton Ampner Baronet, so it seems unlikely that he had already rendered any material services to his country.

Sir Thomas Stewkeley made over Hinton to his son, probably on his marriage, and went to live at a house named Foxleys at Bray. There he died in 1639, aged 70, and was buried in the church there. His widow, however, who survived him for a decade, was buried in the vault at Hinton.

The Stewkeleys were by no means simply country squires, for their connection with the City of London was close ever since, as well as possibly before, Thomas' father had married a daughter of Richard Chamberlayne, Alderman of London. Several left instructions in their wills that if they die in London they are to be buried in one of the City churches, so clearly a large part of their lives was spent in the business centre of England. But what their apparently profitable occupation was, has never been clear, or how they acquired the necessary wealth to buy properties in many different parts of the country. There is no indication that they were merchants, so perhaps they were astute dealers in property.

From an Inquisition taken at the Guildhall in 1640 on the estate of the late Thomas Stewkeley, it appears that he owned extensive property in London. There is particular mention of:

> The whole capital messuage called Northumberland House or Northumberland Place, and also two gardens adjacent to the said messuages, commonly called the Upper Garden and the Lower Garden with all belonging, situate and being in the parish of Sts. Anne and Agnes below Aldersgate London, and 20 messuages, 10 cottages, 30 shops, 10 cellars and 6 gardens with their belongings situated in the parish of Sts. Anne and Agnes Aldersgate.

It is regrettable that none of all this drifted down the centuries to Thomas' descendants. Another investment was an interest in the ferry over the Thames at Fulham. It had been bought by Thomas' father who was Deputy Steward of Fulham in 1546, and bequeathed to his second son, George. On George's death in 1606 it passed to Thomas, who sold his share soon after. Clearly the Stewkeley family had many and varied financial interests.

During the disturbed years leading to the outbreak of the Civil War Stewkeley entries, principally baptism of the children of Sir Hugh, continue to appear, but on 27th September 1642, a month after King Charles raised his standard at Nottingham, the baronet died at the early age of 38 leaving his widow and three young children in the Manor House. Two years later Lady Stewkeley was to find herself in uncomfortable proximity to the engagement which, according to Clarendon 'broke all the measures and altered the whole scheme of the King's counsels'.

From the third week in March 1644 it became clear that there would have to be a decisive engagement between the Cavaliers under Lord Hopton, quartered in and around Winchester, and the Roundheads under Sir William Waller who were advancing through Surrey into Hampshire. By the 25th of the month the London Brigade, which represented the greater part of Waller's troops, had reached the village of West Meon and had already had a number of skirmishes with the King's men, but it was not until the 28th that the two armies, each consisting of about 10,000 men, were poised for the engagement which came to be known as the Battle of Cheriton. The Cavaliers were massed on the high ground south of Alresford and the Roundheads were on the long Lamborough ridge across the valley on the north side of Hinton. From the windows of the house the unfortunate Lady Stewkeley could have had an almost grandstand view of the battle which began at ten in the morning of the 29th amongst the hedges and coppices on the undulations which lay between the two armies. Before nightfall the Cavaliers had been defeated with such great losses that Lamborough Lane is said to have run with blood. It was a defeat from which the King's cause never recovered. But in London the news was received with the utmost joy; and the House of Commons ordered that 9th April should be celebrated as a day of public thanksgiving.

While the Cavaliers were being so bloodily defeated at Cheriton, Winchester Castle, from which a large part of the troops had sallied forth, was held by Sir William Ogle and a garrison. Their position, following the outcome of the battle, was almost hopeless, but for a year and a half they held out in spite of constant attacks, and it was not till 5th October 1645 that in the face of a determined siege they surrendered. General Ogle was well treated by Cromwell, for he and his officers were allowed to leave for Woodstock, while the men dispersed to their homes. It was indeed in some ways a highly gentlemanly war.

As a reward for his heroic resistance the King created Ogle Viscount Ogle of Catherlough in Ireland on the 23rd December 1645. This was no more than a small compensation for the grave reverses the general had suffered. His wife, who had been in the Castle with her husband, had been allowed to leave, but died on the day of surrender at Stoke Charity a few miles from Winchester, the unfortunate Ogle thus not only losing his wife but also 'one thousand pounds a year with her'. A double blow, but one he remedied to some degree about two and a half years later by marrying the widowed Lady Stewkeley. Whether the ceremony took place at Hinton, it is impossible to say for there are no entries of any sort in the Parish Registers after September 1644 until the same month four years later when the following note appears:

> 'ffrances Goodwin M^r of Arts of Trinity College in Cambridge took possession of ye Paris Church of Hinton Almner.'

The entries then begin again, and one must presume that during the interim the Hinton flock had been without a shepherd.

The lives of the newly married couple in those disturbed times were clearly not easy. In November 1646 Lord Ogle had been fined £250 as a Compounder, the sum being assessed at one-tenth of his assets, and his finances do not seem to have rallied from this setback, for in December 1648, the year he married Sarah Stewkeley, he was committed to the Upper Bench prison for debt. Eventually he was released and soon after the Restoration the couple retired together to Lady Ogle's 'jointure house' at Michelmersh, near Romsey, and there Lord Ogle died and was buried in 1682.

I still own the lordship of the manor of Michelmersh—a now empty honour, and all that remains to me of the property which my predecessors acquired there in 1607.

There was another unexpected link between those who took part in the Battle of Cheriton and the family at Hinton. Amongst those captured by the Parliamentarians was Sir Edward Stawell, who was the great uncle of Edward Stawell, who came to live at Hinton 75 years later, having married in 1719 Mary Stewkeley, the granddaughter of the widow who during the battle was sheltering in the Manor House. It is pleasant to learn that both these Cavaliers survived the ordeal of this momentous day and lived well into the reign of Charles II.

The second Sir Hugh, who was only six years of age at the time of the battle, maintained, at least in his first marriage, the family's characteristic of shrewdness by marrying before he was 20 the only daughter and heiress of Sir John Trott, whose property of Laverstoke in the north of the county she inherited. Of their four children only a daughter survived who succeeded to her mother's estate. Lady Stewkeley died on 21st October 1679 and was buried at Laverstoke. The inscription on her monument, which is now in Hinton Church and which I have already described, suggests that she had a rather difficult character, that is to say if one reads correctly between the lines. The anonymous author, who cannot I think have been the bereaved husband, described her character in the following terms:

> She was equall to the Wisdom of the bravest of Men
> Friendlie to the Ignorance of the meanest of women
> Yet she was not altogether exempt from the
> Comon Fate w$\underline{^{ch}}$ attends all Eminencie of Parts
> Of being in some things misunderstood

The author, having thus pronounced his rather equivocal praise, breaks into verse:

> *What certain Judgement can the Vulgar make*
> *Where in the Wise w$\underline{^{th}}$ all their Art mistake*
> *Those of mean Parts uncensured life and Dye*
> *They've nothing to provoke an Envious Eye*
>
> > *The Dull oblige Mankind*
> > *And all their Love engage*
> > *Whilst tis a Crime to be refined*
> > *Above the present Age.*

Above these lines, inscribed on the page of a marble book, the bust of Katherine Stewkeley looks out haughtily from her black-painted niche. There seems little doubt from this inscription that she considered herself the mental superior of her probably rather boorish husband. One wonders how she would have felt had she known that her monument was to be brought to join that of her husband in the church at Hinton.

Two years after the death of Katherine, Sir Hugh was married to Mary Young of Exton, a village a few miles to the south of Hinton. The marriage took place at Hinton on 21st December 1681, the Rector adding after the entry in the Church registers his good wishes for the happiness of the union '*Qui splendide et foelisiter vivunt, vivunt peror*'. Probably having been snubbed by the first Lady Stewkeley with her superior airs, he was hoping for a more genial atmosphere at the Manor House under the influence of the squire's new bride.

The second Sir Hugh, who was destined to be the last male representative of the Stewkeleys, is the only one of the family on whose personality any ray of light is thrown beyond bare dates in the registers. This is due to an occasional reference to him in the Verney Memoirs. His uncle, John Stewkeley, had married Cary

Verney, Lady Gardiner as she continued to call herself from her first marriage, who lived with children and step-children at Preshaw, 3 miles from Hinton, a house which John had inherited from his maternal grandmother, Lady Sandys. The references are not very flattering, but Cary makes the best of an obviously rather difficult man: 'He is very good to me, though hee will sometimes lett us understand hee is lord over us. I truly love him very much for his care of my children.' Hugh paid for the schooling of his young cousins and on this account felt justified in choosing the school the boy attended. 'Brother Stewkeley's (he was in fact her nephew by marriage: she did not marry John Stewkeley until 11 years after the first Sir Hugh's death) humour is to love change which is the undoing of boys', wrote Cary to Sir Ralph Verney, 'and my boy loves the place very well wher he is, which I commend in him; my brother's humors and extravagant exprestions I have to sadly felt, but I must smother thim all for my children's good.'

Sir Hugh was clearly becoming increasingly tiresome, and no doubt he did not hesitate to emphasize the fact that this large and improvident family was considerably indebted to his generosity. Their financial position seems to have deteriorated rapidly, and in 1677 Sir Hugh bought the Preshaw estate from his uncle, and John and Cary with their numerous and unsatisfactory brood moved to London. From this time Hugh's name disappears from the Memoirs.

This autocratic character is borne out by his portrait which hangs at Hinton—a three-quarter length by Thomas Hudson, painted probably about 1700. He is handsomely dressed in a blue coat with a golden silk waistcoat buttoned over a prosperous-looking stomach, but his saturnine face looks out fiercely from the canvas, and his black jowl makes his appearance far from prepossessing. As a portrait, however, it gives the impression that it is a faithful likeness.

I have one other faint contact with Sir Hugh. A few years ago a kind lady gave me a scrapbook which had belonged to her lately deceased father, who lived in a neighbouring village. Seeing references to Hinton in the book, he had always intended to give it to me. On the flyleaf of the book was an inscription in a faded sloping hand written probably in the early nineteenth century saying that the papers pasted into the following pages had been found in the old house at Hinton Ampner when it was let to Mrs. Ricketts in 1765.

At last, I hoped, I was to find some documents which would illuminate the characters of the Stewkeley family—letters from husbands to wives, from fathers to children, anything however trivial of a personal sort. For, though in some ways I feel close to the family, perhaps because the bones of so many of them rest in the vault beneath the chancel of the church less than 100 yards from where I write, yet I know almost nothing of what they were really like. But I was to be disappointed. With one exception the many little manuscripts, some apparently in Hugh Stewkeley's hand, consisted entirely of doggerel verses of a political nature often interlarded with Latin tags, many with a violently 'anti-Popery' trend. Some were obviously sent to him by friends who knew his interest in this subject, and were addressed on the back:

> For Sr Hugh Stewkeley Bart.
> at Hinton near Alresford
> in Hampshire.

There are also a number of printed broadsheets showing the same sentiments. Nothing is more obscure and tedious than dead polemics, and all I can gain from them on the personal side is that Sir Hugh was keenly interested in politics and a rabid anti-Catholic.

The one exception in the whole scrapbook to these absurd macaronics is one letter of some slight interest written by Lady Stewkeley, giving a number of domestic injunctions, but there is no indication to whom it is addressed. It probably dates from about 1700. After providing a recipe for making, I suppose, a cake or pudding which starts off: 'half a hundred of curence, half a hundred of fine sugar' she passes on to the more absorbing subject of clothes:

> Pray will y^u do me ye favour to let my tayler take ye lining out of the goune, and make ye goune into a night goun manto [*sic*] and line it with white satin, and lett him take some of ye blew Lining and put into ye petycote to make it fuller. . . . Pray send me somthing to cover a pair of morning stays and silk enough to make ye child a cote.

There is a good deal more in this style before she passes on to order a few things for the house:

Som pieces small and long and midell sices, green bays for yᵉ
window curtins in yᵉ parlor and curtain rings both bras and horn,
yᵉ cases for my bedpost, 2 pare of lased shoes and one pare of slipers
for my self. Mrs. Stewkeley [her daughter presumably] would have
her sleeves mad fatinable if yᵉ can, and a new fationed hood or quaif
which is most worne.

This long list of orders must have come from the second Lady
Stewkeley who was clearly a practical and domestic type, very
different from the first sharer of Sir Hugh's bed who was 'refined
above the present age'.

On 19th July 1719 Sir Hugh died at the mature age of 81 and
was buried at Hinton. He had lived in six reigns as well as through
the years of the Commonwealth and so had experienced some of
the most dramatic events in the history of this country. He had
had eight children, two sons and two daughters by his first wife,
four daughters by his second. Of these there survived at his death
only the four daughters of the second marriage. His daughter
Katherine, of the first, had married at Hinton in 1679 Sir Charles
Shuckburgh, but had died four years later leaving a son and two
daughters. Stewkeley sons were not favoured with long life, for
John Stewkeley's two sons had also died early, so that in the male
line the family ended with Sir Hugh.

The lack of male heirs was at least of benefit to his daughters
who were well provided for in their father's will. The property of
Laverstoke had already gone to the Shuckburgh family, and the
grandson Sir John Shuckburgh is left only a token £100, with
like sums to other Shuckburgh grandchildren. All Sir Hugh's
properties in Hampshire and Somerset were held in trust for his
daughter Mary, who just before her father's death had married
Edward Stawell, of whom more will be said in the following
chapter, while the three younger daughters were left £5,000
apiece 'if and when they marry with the consent of my wife'.
Sarah, the second, married suitably and no doubt received her
bequest firstly to George Townsend, of Donington in Gloucestershire, and secondly to Ellis St. John, of Dogmersfield in Hampshire. Honoria, the fourth, never married so presumably remained
dependent on her family, but Betty, the third, made a marriage
which must have considerably lowered the prestige of the family.
A year after her father's death she married one William Blake,
who had been Sir Hugh's groom. The proviso in the will may

indicate that Sir Hugh had some suspicion of this romance. In any case Betty appears to have received her mother's consent, and with it the £5,000 without which they would have been in penury. Happiness, if indeed it was happiness, was not of long duration, for after three years of marriage Betty Blake died at the age of 37, and six years later William, who was 12 years her senior died as well. By his will he left not only money for the fine monument to his wife and himself in the church at Weeke, near Winchester, but also a fair sum for the building and endowing of a free school at Hinton. His assets having come from Hinton, he no doubt thought they should return there. The school, with nineteenth-century additions, is still the Primary School for the children of Hinton and Bramdean. The Stewkeley family have long since faded into the mists, but the fruits of the misalliance live on and have brought benefits to many generations of children of the locality.

The Eighteenth Century

⟨ℐℐℐℐ⟩

As has been said in the previous chapter, Mary Stewkeley, the heiress to her father's properties, married Edward Stawell at Hinton on 20th April 1719, a few weeks before Sir Hugh Stewkeley's death. Edward was the third and youngest son of Ralph Stawell of Cothelstone in Somerset, who had been created Baron Stawell of Somerton by Charles II in 1682, as some compensation for the loyalty and sufferings of his father, Sir John Stawell during the Civil War.

Sir John, who came from a family of great antiquity in Somerset, had indeed suffered grievously in the King's cause, not only materially but also physically. He was mentioned by Lord Clarendon as 'a gentleman of one of the largest estates that any man possessed in the West; who had from the beginning shewed very great affection to the person of the King, and to the government that was settled, both in Church and State'. After the surrender of Exeter in 1646 to the Parliamentarians he was incarcerated, and deprived of his estates which remained in sequestration from 1645 to 1652 when a part was sold. Meanwhile Sir John was condemned to 'perpetual imprisonment'. In 1653, however, the Council of State, being in an indulgent mood, ordered his release from the Tower of London on condition he did not leave the City. During the following years he constantly petitioned for the return of his estates saying that he had lost £30,000 in the King's cause and this surely was penalty enough. These pleas were unavailing, and Sir John remained living in the greatest penury in London, which he was not allowed to leave.

With the Restoration he was naturally freed and his estates were returned to him, but he received no financial recompense from the new sovereign, who indeed was in no position to reward his father's supporters. Nor could his physical sufferings be remedied for his health had deteriorated badly, and little more than a year after the Restoration he died. His son Ralph revived the family fortunes by a prudent second marriage—his first wife died in 1670—to Abigail Pitt, heiress of the Hartley Wespall estate in Hampshire. There is a handsome monument to her in the church there recording her death in 1692.

Nine years before Abigail's death Ralph Stawell had received a peerage from a grateful monarch as a reward for 'the extraordinary sufferings and eminent merits of Sir John Stawell, of Cothelstone'. There was a great deal more in the citation about Sir John's courage and loyalty, and his 'afflictions and miseries, (being) reduced to the brinke of famine'. The new peer seems to have possessed some of the toughness of his father, for he was bold enough to protest at the cruel treatment meted out to the Duke of Monmouth's supporters. As a reminder that he would be wiser to restrain his views, Judge Jeffries had two of the rebels hung in chains on the gate at Cothelstone.

Lord Stawell died in 1689 leaving three sons, John, William and Edward. John who was 20 at the time of his father's death died four years later, but in this short space of time had almost dissipated the family fortune which his father had so carefully nurtured. His greatest extravagance was the building of a huge house 400 feet in length and 100 feet in depth close to the church at High Ham in Somerset. Now nothing remains of this great edifice, on which over £100,000 was spent, except sundry mounds of earth and some low walling built up of huge squared stones. The greater part of his estates had to be sold to pay for this folly, so that his brother inherited little except the peerage and Cothelstone Manor.

The Stawells, however, were not slow in reviving their fortunes by prudent marriages, and William secured an affluent widow, a certain Mrs. Forster, with whom he acquired the large estate of Aldermaston, on the border of Hampshire and Berkshire. Male heirs, however, again failed, and on William, Lord Stawell's death in 1741, the peerage passed to the third brother, Edward, who, as we have already seen, had obtained for himself a comfortable life by marrying Mary Stewkeley.

Perhaps the ancient Stawell blood was becoming thin, for there is no evidence that any of the three brothers had any particularly good qualities, though judging by the portraits of the two elder, which hang at Hinton, they had been adequately favoured by nature in their appearance; but it must be owned that full-bottomed wigs are inclined to be becoming.

Since one knows little about the lives of the Edward Stawells, and they do not seem to have touched the outer world at any point that has been recorded, it must be supposed that they lived a quiet country life in the old Manor House at Hinton. Honoria Stewkeley, Mary's younger sister, lived with them, but one has the impression that it was not a happy household, and Edward, Lord Stawell, one must conclude, was an unpleasant character. Had he been otherwise it is improbable that the strange happenings which occurred after his death would have been given so sinister an interpretation.

Two children were born to the Stawells, a son, Stewkeley Stawell in 1720, who died of small-pox at Westminster School at the age of 11, and Mary, who was born six years later, and became the heiress of the family.

Mrs. Stawell died in 1740 and was buried at Hinton, but Lord Stawell, as he became in 1741, remained at Hinton with his sister-in-law Honoria. The latter died in December 1754, and the former four months later. Lord Stawell's death was very sudden and the circumstances have been recorded. He was sitting one April evening in the 'little parlour' at Hinton, the room presumably on the west side of the great hall which had windows facing southward over the park. One pictures him as a red-faced, choleric figure with his foot on a gout-stool, and suffering from a blood pressure much heightened by excessive port drinking. He would have been dressed in the rather shabby snuff-coloured coat which was his usual wear. Suddenly he was attacked by a fit of apoplexy, and after mumbling a few words he remained speechless till he died early next morning. On 19th April his body joined those of his wife's ancestors in the vault beneath the church, thus keeping company with the remains of his sister-in-law which had so lately been placed there.

This, however, was not the end of Lord Stawell's and Honoria's connection with this world, but in order to keep the sequence of dates correct it is necessary, before describing their subsequent behaviour, to follow the lives of Lord Stawell's daughter and her husband.

Five years before her father's death, Mary Stawell had married Henry Legge, the fourth son of the 1st Earl of Dartmouth. He was the only person to live at Hinton who was prominent in the world, the only one, indeed, to earn an entry in the *Dictionary of National Biography* where his achievements fill more than two pages. As a fourth son his patrimony must have been small, and he was under the necessity of making his own way in the world. He was fortunate enough at a fairly early age to catch the eye of Sir Robert Walpole whose private secretary he became.

Unfortunately, however, he incurred the enmity of Horace Walpole, Sir Robert's third son, who dipping his pen in vitriol was able to perpetuate his feelings in print in his *Memoir of the Reign of George II*. The following are the blistering words:

> Legge was a younger son of Lord Dartmouth, who had early turned him into the world to make his fortune, which he pursued with uncommon assiduity of duty. Avarice or flattery, application or ingratitude, nothing came amiss that might raise him on the ruins of either friends or enemies; indeed neither were so to him, but by the proportion of their power. He had been introduced to Sir Robert Walpole by his second son, and soon grew an unmeasurable favourite, till endeavouring to steal his patron's daughter, at which in truth Sir Robert's partiality for him seemed to connive, he was discarded entirely, yet taken care of.

He was, in fact, made Surveyor of the King's Woods and Forests, quite a lucrative post, and in 1740 he entered the House of Commons as member for a Cornish borough, until the following year when he was elected for the borough of Orford in Suffolk which he held for 18 years.

No doubt his marriage to the heiress Mary Stawell in 1750 greatly assisted his position, although she did not receive her full inheritance till five years later. But he had good fortune in another, and perhaps unexpected, direction. Under the will of his father's first cousin, Leonard Bilson, he was bequeathed the estate of Mapledurham near Petersfield on condition that he added the name Bilson to his own: a harmless stipulation which entailed also quartering the Legge arms with the curious shield of the Bilsons which consisted of a Tudor rose 'dimidiated' (divided) with a Pomegranate. The estate was part of the manor of Buriton, the remainder of which Henry Bilson-Legge's son later bought from

Edward Gibbon, the historian. It was of Buriton that Gibbon wrote in his autobiography:

> My father's residence in Hampshire, where I have passed many light and some heavy hours, was at Buriton near Petersfield. . . . If strangers had nothing to see, the inhabitants had little to desire.

With his wife's estates and the Bilson property Henry Bilson-Legge was financially well equipped, and with his astute political brain his success was fairly well assured. It was accepted that he was a shrewd man of business and one of the few in the Commons at that time to have a grasp of commercial affairs. In 1759 he gave up the borough of Orford and was elected for Hampshire where he had become a considerable landowner. In this election he defeated Sir Simeon Stuart whose large property at Hartley Mauditt, near Alton, he and his wife later purchased. A double insult perhaps.

His progress in the political world in support of the Whigs was rapid. After being for some years a Lord of the Treasury, he twice became Chancellor of the Exchequer—in the Duke of Newcastle's administration in 1754 and two years later in the Duke of Devonshire's government. In 1760 his wife was created Baroness Stawell with remainder to their heirs male, the purpose of the grant being to do him an honour, but at the same time to retain his services in the Commons. It was improbable that a man so successful should not have detractors, and Lord Holland in his *Memoir* has some bitter words for him which bear out, it must be owned, Horace Walpole's views:

> He sacrificed ev'ry honest consideration . . . to selfish cunning. He has through life no sooner got preferment from one patron, than he look'd to his adversary and probable successor for the preservation or augmentation of it.

Whatever Lord Holland's and Horace Walpole's views may have been, Pitt thought highly of him, and spoke of him as:

> The child, and deservedly the favourite child, of the Whigs.

and even Horace Walpole admitted that speaking against the tax on plate:

> Legge alone shone: he entered beyond his usual brevity, into a detail of the nature of coin, exchange, gold, silver, premiums, and the mistaken or real advantages of those manufactures.

Financial aptitude was perhaps his strong suit rather than loyalty.

He died in 1764, aged 56, and was buried at Hinton where the inscription on his monument, not unexpectedly, presents a happier picture of his, perhaps ambivalent, character. After a fulsome description of his achievements in public life, it continues:

> In private life he possessed every amiable and respectable
>   quality;
> Great without pride, and good without ostentation;
> Humane, benevolent, condescending,
> Sincere in his friendship, ardent in his affections
> Engaging in his address, instructive in his conversation
> Wherein extensive knowledge, just reflection, and exquisite
>   sentiment, were enforced with all the powers of language,
> And enlivened with a peculiar vein of the most striking wit.

Indeed in death he clearly shone as a paragon endowed with every virtue of character, and let us suppose it was only political animosity which prompted some of his contemporaries to see him in an unfavourable light.

In the Church Register his burial is recorded on 5th September without comment, and this simple entry without flourish clearly incensed a subsequent rector, who in 1792 wrote the following note on the opposite page:

> The Right Honble Henry Bilson-Legge, one of the most upright public characters and able men in the Kingdom; whose death ought not to have been thus entered in the Register *equally mentioned* by Dr. Durnford with that of his old servant Joseph Silly immediately preceding it.

Perhaps Dr. Durnford belong to the Horace Walpole faction.

In his will Henry Bilson-Legge bequeathed to his wife 'Jewels, Plate, Linnen, Furniture, China and Household goods in any of my houses', and all the remainder to his son Henry Stawell Bilson-Legge when 21. His widow was 38 years old at the time of his death, and after a decent pause of four years, she married as his second wife the Earl of Hillsborough, who after her death was created Marquis of Downshire.

Mary Stawell may not have had happy memories of her childhood at Hinton, and it seems that she and her husband seldom came there after her father's death, their visits usually being confined to a few weeks in the autumn for the shooting. Whether these visits were altogether pleasant has not been recorded. In any case after Henry Bilson-Legge's death, Lady Stawell at once decided to let the house. Suitable tenants were soon found in Mr. and Mrs. Ricketts, who with their family moved in in January 1765, the house apparently being let fully furnished, but most of their retainers they brought with them from their house in London.

No place could have been apparently more peaceful or better suited to the bringing up of a family of small children, but almost immediately Mr. and Mrs. Ricketts found that there was something curious, something inexplicable, about the house. Their nights were much disturbed by the sounds of the opening and shutting of doors, and Mrs. Ricketts feared that 'irregularities' were going on amongst the servants. However, inspection by Mr. Ricketts showed that all was in order. Another possible solution was that someone had keys of the house and came in and out at night. Accordingly all the locks were changed, but without effect on the nocturnal noises. Mrs. Ricketts was a woman of great strength of mind, but one senses that the nerves of the household were getting a little on edge, and one wonders whether the unexplained figures they saw on several occasions were not the product of over-excited imaginations. Two different men saw a figure in a snuff-coloured coat, once inside the house and once outside, while the assembled servants sitting in the kitchen saw a tall woman in a dark, rustling silk dress rush through the room and out into the yard, but a man coming in at that moment through the yard had seen no one. It was all very baffling.

However, after a time the manifestations seem to have quietened down a little, and at the end of 1769 Mr. Ricketts left without anxiety to visit his property in Jamaica, leaving his wife with three children and eight servants at Hinton. The relief was not of long duration, and soon the strange sounds began again with renewed vigour. Mrs. Ricketts kept an exact record of all she heard and felt, and included the names of her servants who were all changed from those who had come with her from London. It is this careful account which makes the Hinton ghost story one of the best recorded of the eighteenth century.

In the summer of 1770 she noted that when 'lying in the yellow bedchamber'—a room in the centre of the north side of the house

—'I plainly heard the footsteps of a man, with plodding step, walking towards the foot of my bed.' She sprang out of bed and rushed into the adjoining nursery and returned with the nurse and a light, but there was no one to be found. This alarming sort of manifestation was repeated not only in her room but also in the room of her maid who also stated that she heard 'dismal groans and fluttering' round her bed. Another strange sound was 'a hollow murmuring that seemed to possess the whole house; it was independent of wind, being equally heard on the calmest nights'.

Disturbing noises continued almost nightly though they varied in degree and also in style. One night, for example, the front door was heard to slam with such violence that Mrs. Ricketts' bedroom above the hall shook 'perceivably'. But 'upon examining the door it was found fast locked and bolted as usual'. As the summer advanced the disturbances became more intolerable. 'They began before I went to bed, and with intermissions were heard till after broad day in the morning.' Human voices now joined the general cacophony: 'a shrill female voice would begin, and then two others with deeper and manlike tone seemed to join in the discourse'. One night when in her bedroom, where her maid also slept, she had a particularly terrifying experience: 'I heard the most loud, deep tremendous noise, which seemed to rush and fall with infinite velocity and force on the lobby floor.' This was instantly followed by 'a shrill and dreadful shriek . . . repeated three or four times'.

The situation was clearly getting out of hand and Mrs. Rickett's health, and no doubt that of her maids, was beginning to suffer. The continued absence of her husband robbed her of her natural support, but fortunately just as matters were becoming desperate, her brother Admiral Jervis, later Earl of St. Vincent, sailed into Portsmouth and from that place came to stay at Hinton. The story in all its alarming details was told to him, and he decided to sit up for several nights with a friend, Mr. Luttrell, expecting no doubt that the manifestation were due to some human agency, and that they would capture any malefactors bold enough to carry on their nocturnal activities. The two watchers settled down for the night in different rooms, but before an hour or two had passed the usual sounds of footsteps and banging doors were heard in passages and lobbies. They immediately rushed out of their respective rooms, pistols in hand, to find nothing except each other. The Hinton ghosts, indeed, were not ones to be discouraged by a distinguished sailor and his friend.

Admiral Jervis insisted that his sister and her family should leave the haunted house as soon as possible, and they soon moved to Wolvesey at Winchester, which was offered to them by the Bishop. Soon after she took a house in London, but she did not lose her connection with Hinton, for on Mr. Ricketts' return to England they rented the 'Parsonage' for two years since they were anxious to keep the farm at Hinton which they had leased. In November 1771 Admiral Jervis wrote to Mrs. Ricketts:

> My dear sister's comfortable letter dated Wolsey Sept. 2nd. . . . I never was more rejoiced at any event than I am to know you are retired from Hinton and that you are likely to get rid of it entirely on such favourable terms, at the same time I highly approve your attention to Lady Stawell.

A month later he wrote again, on this occasion from Pisa:

> I wait impatiently for the revealment of this Hinton unsearchable Business and beg you will be particular in every circumstance.

His sister's situation was obviously always in his mind, and early in the following year he wrote:

> The Duke (of Gloucester) frequently asks if I have heard any more of the Hinton mystery and interests himself greatly in your sufferings which I most ardently wish may soon be put an end to by a manifest discovery of the cause of your disturbance.

By April 1772 the family had moved to London and the Rectory had been rented, for the Admiral's letter from Rome of that date is addressed to Curzon Street:

> The addition of expense in renting the Parsonage House is not to be put into competition with your peace of mind.

No 'revealment' was ever forthcoming in spite of the offer of a reward of £100 made by Lady Stawell and Mr. Ricketts jointly to anyone who could solve the mystery. There is no record that any attempt was made to exorcize the house, and it is surprising that Mrs. Ricketts, who had an extensive acquaintance amongst the bench of bishops, did not call in one of these heavyweights to attack the ghosts.

Lady Stawell, who by this time had married her second husband Lord Hillsborough, apparently raised no objection to the surrender of the lease, and one wonders whether, during her visits to Hinton during her first husband's life-time, she had perhaps been subjected to these supernatural disturbances. Lady Hillsborough died in 1780 and her coffin joined that of her first husband in the vault at Hinton. She left an only son to succeed to her property and to her title of Stawell. The sinister Manor House must have remained practically deserted, except for the ghosts. But not entirely, seemingly, for my grandmother made the following note at the end of a printed record of the ghost story:

> My mother-in-law [Lady Sherborne] remembers when about 6 years old [*c.* 1786] while staying at Hinton being awoke in the night and carried down to the Rectory as the noises were so great Lady Stawell could not remain in the house.

A house so uninhabitable was clearly useless, and also no doubt was falling into disrepair, so in 1793 Lord Stawell decided to pull it down and rebuild on a slightly different site. When the house was demolished a box was found under one of the floors. In the box was a small skull optimistically said to be that of a monkey. In any case it was at once removed by the Steward of the estate, and nothing was heard of it again; but the find was taken as proof of a story that had long circulated in the neighbourhood that the ghosts were those of Edward, Lord Stawell and his sister-in-law, Honoria Stewkeley, and that they had done away with a little bastard that they had produced between them. But the truth will never be known.

The last years of the Tudor house were the saddest that Hinton has ever known. The sinister, deserted building with its surroundings, probably barely maintained, must have presented a spectacle of the utmost gloom to those who came to worship in the little church, which was only separated from it by a few yards. Perhaps it was a warning of the effects of wickedness, and so an inducement to piety, but in any case the condition of the house inevitably presented a dismal contrast to its appearance when it was inhabited by the prosperous Stewkeleys and their large families in the early years of the century.

Henry Stawell Bilson-Legge succeeded on his mother's death as the 2nd Baron Stawell of the second creation. He was an only child, born in 1757, seven years after his parents' marriage. In his portrait by Daniel Gardner, painted when he was about 20, he appears as a handsome and agreeable-looking young man. But Gardner's popularity as a portrait painter stemmed no doubt from his ability to impart to his sitters a high degree of grace and beauty, while at the same time presenting a fairly close likeness. It was a useful gift, shared by a number of the fashionable portrait painters of the latter part of the eighteenth century.

In this picture Henry, Lord Stawell, stands in a woodland glade and is elegantly dressed in a crimson coat, with black breeches and white stockings, while his powdered hair is tied back behind his head. In his right hand he holds a tricorn hat, and his left rests on the head of a dog which appears to be a cross between a wolf and a jackal. Gardner's flattery and gift for portraiture evidently did not extend to animals. This was Henry as a young man: I had also a portrait, painted when he was about 60 years old, a cheap likeness, I would say, perhaps done by some itinerant artist. He was no Dorian Gray. The well-cut features, which Gardner had observed, had disappeared into a round fleshy face, in which were set small, cunning-looking eyes. The powdered hair had diminished to some sparse strands, and the whole head seemed to have sunk into the shoulders without perceptible neck. Neither the quality of the painting nor the character portrayed made it a pleasant work, and one wonders that the sitter did not destroy it. However, it was one of the less regretted losses in the flames of 1960.

It seems probable that the itinerant artist had come nearer to the character of his sitter than the accomplished Daniel Gardner, unless 40 years of life had made a radical change, for Henry Stawell does not appear to have been an amiable person. He was a friend of some intimacy of the Prince Regent, though this might have been as much to his credit as the reverse, but the lawsuits and quarrels in which he seems constantly to have been engaged with people of all ranks hardly suggests that he was particularly agreeable.

A typical case is mentioned by Gilbert White in his *Natural History of Selborne* in connection with Alice Holt Forest, the Rangership of which Lord Stawell had inherited from his mother, and the timber in which he claimed as his own:

The poor of the parishes of Binsted and Frinsham, Bentley and

Kingsley, assert that it (the lop and top) belongs to them; and, assembling in a riotous manner, have actually taken it all away. . . . Forty-five of these people his Lordship has served with actions.

It must be owned that Lord Stawell had the Law on his side, for in the grant of the Rangership from the Crown to his mother in 1766, and later confirmed to himself, it was expressly stated that the rights included:

> To have and to take all beasts or animals attached or taken within the said forest or chase, by any of the foresters there and all manner of wood blown or thrown down by the wind and all dead wood etc and housebote and firebote.

The two last mysterious words indicate, I think, timber suitable for repairs to buildings and firewood, so that the villagers had little justification for their claim, but in any case it would have been more gracious to give way—at no personal expense—to his poor neighbours; but charity was apparently not one of Henry Stawell's qualities. His passion was hunting, and for this pursuit the Rangership of the Forest was particularly propitious. Thus he lived for a great part of his life either at the Great Lodge in the Forest or a few miles away at a house called Marelands close to the village of Bentley. His hounds he kept at the Great Lodge and there also he had his stud of racehorses with which he had considerable success, on one occasion winning the Derby with his horse Blücher.

A caustic reference to Lord Stawell, which shows little love or respect, was made by the Vicar of Bentley in 1793:

> My noble neighbour, Lord S., has lately taken it into his head to act as Justice of the Peace, but before he is qualified to enter upon the execution of his office he is, by Act of Parliament, obliged to give public testimony of his faith by receiving the Sacrement of the Lord's Supper in the face of the congregation. He made his appearance this morning.

He married when he was 22, and, one hopes, still looking like the Gardner portrait, Mary Curzon, daughter of Viscount Curzon of Penn, who was then 19. One has the impression that they were both difficult people. The tradition that Lord Stawell demolished the house on his property at Hartley Mauditt because his wife wished to live in it, hardly suggests a very harmonious *ménage*.

They had, however, two children, a daughter Mary, born a year after their marriage, who was my great-grandmother, and a son Henry who, in the tradition of the heirs of the Stewkeleys, Stawells and Legges, died at the age of three years and was buried in the vault at Hinton. Lord Stawell held only one public office, that of 'Patent Surveyor of the Customs in the Port of London'. What exactly this indicated I do not know, but I would suppose it was a well-paid sinecure—perhaps obtained for him by his father.

Whatever Henry Stawell's shortcomings, and nature seems to have provided him with rather more than the normal ration, I feel grateful to him on two counts. Firstly for having bought some attractive silver of good late eighteenth-century design, part of which, engraved with an 'S' surmounted by a coronet, has descended into my possession; and secondly, and far more important, for having built in 1793 the house which forms the nucleus of the building in which I am now writing. It is not so much for what he built, for that was fairly commonplace, but for where he built it. The choice of site, indeed, shows great perception.

The haunted Tudor house, as has already been said, stood next the church on the very crest of the low ridge, where it was fully exposed to every wind that blew across this rather windswept county. The new site lay 60 yards or so to the south so that trees planted on the north and east sides provide shelter from the coldest winds, while by turning the house very slightly to the west of due south it not only gets almost all possible sunshine, but also stands at that point from which the landscape composes most happily.

Whether these considerations were in Lord Stawell's mind when he chose the new site, or whether he merely wished to leave the piece of ground on which his ancestors had made so great a nuisance of themselves, it is impossible to say, but whatever the reason my gratitude remains. There is one small drawback to the slight change of aspect: it has meant that the three features which still survive from the Tudor house are on a different axis to the present building. These features are the kitchen garden, the stables, and the remains of the old lime avenue which extended southward from the front door. It cannot be said that this is a great drawback, but it entails, for example, the drive, which my parents made down to the main road in the valley on the north, approaching the house at a somewhat oblique angle although running parallel with the kitchen-garden wall.

The stables, which are the oldest building surviving at Hinton, may perhaps be allowed to receive a short reference here. In their present appearance—a long brick building with a tiled roof, and a tall central doorway flanked on either side by three casement windows—they would seem to date from about 1700. But the southern end in which the ceiling is supported by massive ships' timbers must date from an earlier period, and it is probable that an existing stable was enlarged by Sir Hugh Stewkeley, who made his addition into one modest composition with the old and built a rudimentary pediment over the central door to give the building a little style.

When I was young the stables were, of course, well filled with horses. At the north end, in a roomy loose box, was my father's hunter already more or less in retirement, then came two modern loose boxes for the children's ponies, while the two carriage horses had agreeable rooms in other parts of the building. This left two stalls for any visiting horses, in which the original arrangements for feeding survived—iron mangers and wooden racks into which hay could be pushed down from the loft above. At the south end of the block was the coachhouse which contained a brougham, two waggonettes—large and small—a dogcart or two, and what I think was known as a governess cart in which we children took our outings under the supervision, indeed, of a governess. This was quite a modest set-up for the period; in a horsy household the installation would have been far greater.

On the west side of the stable building was the harness-room with windows looking out on to the stable yard. This was the particular preserve of the coachman and the grooms, and all others were encouraged to keep out. The coachman was a strong believer in the strap for exercising discipline on his sons of whom the younger, Tommy, was particularly obstreperous. The necessary correction often took place in the harness-room where straps were conveniently at hand, and shrill cries would echo into the yard. But I do not think Tommy was much hurt as he would emerge after the operation a trifle flushed but looking quite cheerful.

While the Tudor house existed the stable buildings lay at right angles and to the south-west of it; when the Georgian house rose on the site further south the stables came to the north-west and were at a slightly obtuse angle to it. And thus it remains as the house is today.

The new house was simple and straightforward. It was solidly built in a pale yellow brick and was fairly spacious, but it would seem that Lord Stawell expended little money on elaborate decoration. It consisted of a square block with a pedimented doorway on the north with a single window on either side. On the south there were five windows on the ground and first floor while behind the parapet which ran round the house were dormer windows in the mansard roof. These details I know from a very few surviving photographs taken by my grandmother about 1860 and also from the aquatint of the Hampshire Hunt, which is dated 1819 and shows the house in the background. On the west of the main block was a long wing containing kitchens and so forth, and also a brewhouse, but neither the photographs nor the aquatint show these buildings very clearly. Although my father lived in the house for some years when he was young, he had no precise memory of how it was planned. On the east side there was apparently a double drawing-room divided by folding doors and with windows south and east, and the remainder of the south front was taken up by the dining-room. The staircase seems to have risen on the west side of the front hall, and beyond the stair was a small room facing north. On the two floors above there must have been nine or ten bedrooms.

It was the sort of house, indeed, which is now looked on as 'desirable', for without being large it must have had a certain dignity, and once the service arrangements in the wing had been curtailed would have been very workable. The contents of the Tudor house, such as survived, were presumably transferred to the new building, and Lord Stawell, like his father, used it rather occasionally when he came to shoot over the estate.

In 1820 Henry, Lord Stawell, died at his house in Grosvenor Place in London, and with him the peerage expired for the second time. It can hardly be said that any of the men who had held the peerage, with the exception of the first, had possessed either worth or distinction. Like his predecessors he was buried at Hinton, the last to enter the vault under the chancel. He was the fifth owner of Hinton to be buried there since Sir Hugh Stewkeley had been interred in 1642, while the majority of widows and a great number of children had joined their respective spouses and parents, so that the crowd must be considerable. It is curious that however neglectful of Hinton they may have been in their lives, they remained faithful to it in death.

Lord Stawell's will, or rather the codicils, are revealing. The will, dated 12th September 1810, contains no surprises. All the properties which his father had inherited from Leonard Bilson, and which seem to have included Marelands near Bentley, as well as Mapledurham, near Petersfield, went under the entail to the son of his uncle Heneage Legge, and all the remainder of his property was bequeathed to his daughter, and only surviving child, Mary, wife of John Dutton.

All this was highly correct and proper; but on the same day he made a codicil leaving an annuity of £200 to Elizabeth Crowe of No. 9 Vauxhall Walk, Lambeth. A generous gesture to an old servant, one kindly thinks, until one finds that two years later Mrs. Hodges, who appears to have neither Christian name nor address, is to receive a princely annuity of £400 with all her debts paid. By the same codicil Mrs. Moseley receives £1,000 'as a mark of the great regard and pure friendship I bear her'. In 1816 Jane Evans of Fulham is rewarded with £300 a year 'and all my Exchequer Bills'. And lastly a year before he died 'Facimia Groves, my personal servant now living with me', is bequeathed an annuity of £100. It is pleasant to know that the women who cherished him during his declining years were so handsomely provided for. It cannot have been an altogether agreeable occupation, and one trusts he was equally lavish to them in life.

On the death of her brother at the age of three years, Mary Legge had become an extremely eligible young woman, and as she grew up, came to be known appropriately as 'the Hampshire Heiress'. The properties she inherited from her father must have extended to between 10,000 and 15,000 acres. In addition to Hinton, there were the Hartley Mauditt and Kingsley estates near Alton, Timsbury and Michelmersh near Romsey, and Bedhampton near Havant. Also there was a property at Wootton Courtney in Somerset, which had remained in the family from the time of the Stewkeleys. Of all these properties, Hinton was the smallest, and is the only one which has survived the depredations of death duties and other difficulties.

Victorian Comfort and Beauty

Mary Bilson-Legge, the Hampshire Heiress, must have been a highly sought after young woman, but she was 23 years old before my great-grandfather, John Dutton, persuaded her to fall into his arms. How he secured this prize, I do not know, but it was anyhow a case of money marrying money for John was the only son of the 1st Baron Sherborne and heir to very large properties in Gloucestershire. This wealthy couple were married with some pomp at St. George's, Hanover Square, on 11th August 1803, and their marriage lasted, happily so far as I know, for 59 years.

The last Lord Stawell, Mary Bilson-Legge's father, had died in 1820, and for 30 years or so following his death the personal connection of the family with Hinton was slight. At some time anything which appeared of family interest was removed to Sherborne; this included pictures, miniatures, plate and the Stawell diamonds. But the furniture seems to have disappeared, and no doubt it was considered old fashioned and not worth transferring the 80 miles or so to Gloucestershire. Even before Lord Stawell's death the house appears to have been often let, since in the aquatint dated 1819 of the Hampshire Hounds meeting in the park on the south side of the house Hinton is called 'The Seat of R. Heysham Esq.'. And earlier in the century a family named Kingscote was in the house for some years. The baptisms of several children appear in the Registers, also there is a small marble slab in the floor of the church nave close to the pulpit commemorating Louisa Frances Kingscote who was born and who died on the same day, 22nd February 1804.

But a tenant for much the longest space was Mrs. Augustus Legge, the widow of the 5th son of the 2nd Earl of Dartmouth, and so a near cousin to my great-grandmother, the owner. In

1822 she presented the stained glass in the pair of tall lancet windows at the east end of the church. In their crude colouring and repetitive pattern they seem now an unfortunate choice, but perhaps having once been admired they will be so again. She was probably well established in the house at that date, and she is recorded as still being the tenant of Lord Sherborne on the Tithe Map of 1839. She did not die till 1863 and may have remained as a tenant until near the time when my grandparents came to inhabit the house in 1857.

There is no reason to suppose that my great-grandfather ever came to Hinton, and certainly no building of any sort was carried out during the lives of himself and his wife. On the Hartley Mauditt property, however, several cottages were built about 1835, so as a landlord he was not entirely neglectful.

My great-grandparents had three sons, James, born in 1804; John, my grandfather, in 1810; and Ralph in 1821. It seems to have been early decided that the two younger sons would divide their mother's property on her death, John to inherit Hinton and Hartley Mauditt, Ralph, Timsbury and Bedhampton. It was a happy and amicable arrangement. Fortified by this prospect, my grandfather married in 1836 the more or less penniless daughter of the 5th Earl of Macclesfield.

This would have seemed a suitable occasion for the young couple to move to Hinton, which was eventually to be their property, but no, they continued to live at Sherborne with John's parents. The house is enormous, but nevertheless it seems strange that they did not wish for an establishment of their own. However, John had been born at Sherborne, he had spent his youth there, and he remained there. His obedient Lavinia raised, I suppose, no objection.

They were a completely compatible couple, and serious discord was I believe unknown, but there was one major reverse—the years passed and no children were born to them. At last after ten years of barren marriage they decided to try the waters of Bad Kissingen, which had an international reputation as an aid to fertility. My grandfather kept a diary of the journey. They left England soon after Christmas 1845, travelling in their own carriage and accompanied by a courier. This was as far as comfort went: the roads, the inns, the drunken postilions must have made the journey to our ideas a nightmare.

However, they arrived at last and settled down for a few months of curative water-drinking. In April, with joy, my grandfather was able to write in large capital letters in his diary 'Lavinia is with child'. This might have seemed a prudent moment to return home, but no, they decided to rattle away across the Alps and spend the summer in Italy, in Florence, Rome and Naples. In the late autumn they returned to Bad Kissingen, Lavinia fortunately still with child, and after a further spell with the waters there, they returned to England. The journey, one would have supposed, would have been dangerous for someone in my grandmother's condition, but it was successfully achieved, though with not much time to spare. They reached England at the end of the year, and on 17th January 1847 my father came into the world.

He was born in London, but the family soon returned to Sherborne and continued living there for another ten years during which time four children were born to them of whom one daughter died at the age of one year. My uncle, the last child, was born in 1857, the year in which they eventually transferred to Hinton, and it may have been this addition which finally decided them to make the move.

Although my grandfather did not inherit Hinton till his mother's death in 1864, he began in the '50s making journeys to Hinton, presumably in order to keep an eye on the estate. He made short entries in his very unilluminating diary 'to Hinton', and a day or two later 'home again'. The house must have been available for these visits, but perhaps was only rudimentarily furnished.

I personally feel so much part of Hampshire, that I find it difficult to understand my grandparents' apparent reluctance to leave Gloucestershire. But it was perhaps natural. My grandfather had lived all his life at Sherborne, my grandmother came from the neighbouring county of Oxfordshire, many relations lived in the area, so that leaving the wide spaces of the rolling Cotswold hills for the rather small-scale landscape of Hampshire may have seemed like moving into a foreign country.

It was not only the landscape which was small-scale: there was also the house. To leave the palatial environment of Sherborne with its great stone-pillared Renaissance façade and endless rooms for the modest yellow brick box at Hinton, must have seemed a rude descent in the social scale, and they may have felt that their standing in their new county would be far lower than in the one they were leaving. This is, of course, surmise, but social values were important considerations in the nineteenth century.

The style too of Hinton was, in 1857, about as far out of fashion as it could be. The Great Exhibition was only a few years in the past, and the influence of the taste there shown was constantly growing. Elaboration and decoration were highly admired, and the simple, rectangular lines of Hinton must have seemed bleak indeed. However, John and Lavinia were not very well-off, and the restricted size of the house was well suited to the scale of their assets.

The house had to be furnished, and they were able, with some difficulty, I believe, to obtain from Lady Sherborne some of the pictures and other objects which had belonged to her family and had come from Hinton. There was the portrait of Sir Hugh Stewkeley by Hudson, very conventional portraits by Dahl of the 2nd and 3rd Lords Stawell, some pictures of the last Lord Stawell's racehorses and so forth. But a charming portrait of Mary Bilson-Legge as a child by Opie, and a handsome picture of Henry Bilson-Legge in his robes as Chancellor of the Exchequer by William Hoare my great-grandparents were unwilling to part with. The Opie is now in America and the Hoare still hangs at Sherborne. However, to make up for these omissions, my grandparents were sent off with some silver, a few diamonds, and a number of miniatures. Thus with these mementoes of their predecessors at Hinton they set up their modest establishment.

My grandmother's activities in photography, still a fairly new amusement in the 1860s, were generally confined to outdoor subjects, romantic views and so forth which, though technically excellent, are not of much interest today. However, she was successful in taking one time-exposure of the drawing-room at Hinton. From the appearance of the room the family would seem to have been installed for several years, so I would suppose it dates from 1862 or 63. My grandmother had obviously achieved that first requisite for a mid-Victorian room—fullness. It appears to have been crammed with little tables, wood-framed semi-easy chairs, china ornaments heaped on *étagères*, whatnots and so forth, while the windows were well draped with curtains and the simple marble chimney-piece was partly concealed by a heavy pelmet on a mantel-board. The room had perhaps a certain cosy charm,

but there was nothing in it of the remotest value, and I am inclined
to doubt whether 'artistic' visitors looked on it as a satisfactory
example of contemporary style.

I imagine that during these first years at Hinton my grandfather
spent much time considering how he would convert his plain,
moderate-sized house into something more suited to the taste of
the period so soon as circumstances allowed. This, of course,
meant the death of his mother, when the Hinton and Hartley
Mauditt properties would come into his possession and provide
him with a satisfactory income. They were much the same sentiments as possessed his grandson 75 years later.

Lady Sherborne died in 1864 and was buried at Sherborne,
being the only one out of eight owners of Hinton from Sir Hugh
Stewkeley to my father who was not buried either in the vault or
the churchyard. My grandfather, now in a happy position of
comparative affluence, seems to have lost no time about considering plans for transforming the house. It was not, however, without
great thought that the final design for the monstrosity which arose
was reached. As with Sir Christopher Wren at St. Paul's, it was
the third design which was finally accepted.

The first intention was to demolish the existing house entirely,
and to start afresh on the same site. With these instructions, plans
were produced by a competent architect, but unfortunately his
name nowhere appears on his designs. The house he proposed consisted of a large main block of three floors, with six reception rooms
on the ground floor, to this was connected by a narrow neck, a
spreading service wing built round an open courtyard. The whole
was to be built of brick with a slate roof, but it is difficult to say
what style of architecture it was intended to represent. There was a
slight Tudor flavour, although the plate-glass windows prevented
it from being a very successful essay in that manner, but at least
it had the complete lack of symmetry or even of balance, which
was much admired at the time.

In order to persuade a possibly doubtful client, the architect
produced a large and attractive watercolour. The house itself
was no doubt drawn in his office and the picture was then handed
over to an artist for the purpose of softening and embellishing the
rigid lines of the structure. The building thus rose from agreeable
bosky surroundings of trees and shrubberies, while a landau and
pair at the entrance with a liveried footman on the door-step and

a few crinolined figures drifting along the drive, indicated clearly how delightful life could be in the house if built. These blandishments, however, my grandfather resisted. Possibly he felt that the 40 or so bedrooms that the proposed house would contain were slightly beyond his financial status. Anyhow the plans were rejected, and it was necessary to start again.

The second design seems to have come from another hand, although here again there is no name on the plans, but the presentation was simpler and the architecture very different. Once again, however, the design came from an architect who knew what he was about, and the plans showed a perfectly workable building. His suggestion was to retain the existing house, to add a large drawing-room to it at the east end, a dining-room and a very long service wing on the west. The architecture was to be Ruskinian Gothic with tall, pointed windows flanked by marble, or stone pillars. The straightforward lines of the Georgian house were to be cleverly concealed behind this elaborate Gothic cloak. The architect, whoever he was, had clearly lately read and well digested *The Stones of Venice* which had been published some years earlier.

Once again, however, my grandfather was not satisfied, and the plans were rejected, but on what grounds I do not know. He then decided to abandon architects altogether, and to employ simply a capable builder. His choice fell on a Mr. Kemp, of Alton, who had erected a number of particularly hideous buildings in the neighbourhood. Purely as a builder there was nothing amiss with his work: as a planner and designer his ignorance was abysmal, and I fear I should add that my grandparents cannot have been much better.

My grandfather's instruction to Mr. Kemp were apparently simple: there must be a large drawing-room—my grandmother insisted on this—a very high kitchen, about 30 bedrooms all told, and no bathroom. The last injunction was important: my grandfather had once caught cold in one of these new-fangled contraptions and there was to be nothing of the sort in his house. Mr. Kemp was then obviously shown the 'second' plan in order to provide him with a few ideas. Had he copied this plan more closely, the house would not have been so disastrously inconvenient.

Following his instructions Mr. Kemp planned a large double

drawing-room at the east end of the house, the whole of the north side of the existing house was made into an entrance hall with a new stair at the west end, while the two rooms on the south side were a library and a dining-room, the latter enlarged by throwing out a bow-window to the south and a deep recess bulging into the hall to the north. Then came a long, long, 'L'-shaped service wing. The style of architecture adopted was, I think, Tudor. The heavily stone-mullioned windows would seem to have indicated this intention, and this was borne out by the gables with heavy wooden bargeboards, and the battlements surmounting the bow windows. The whole was solidly built in brick, red stretchers and blue headers, with dark blue pointing. This was intended, no doubt, to give an air of antiquity but in effect produced an apoplectic colour little relieved by stone quoins and a stone Tudor-esque moulding which ran round the main part of the house below the first-floor windows.

In front of the house a spacious gravelled forecourt was dug out of the ground, which sloped slightly upwards on the north side. Into this a new porch, with a three-sided bay-window on the first floor, projected and the front door was reached by a rather well-arranged flight of five or six steps. The date on the rain-water heads was 1867, a middle date I would suppose between beginning and completing, for the whole operation took between two and three years, during which time my grandparents lived in a rented house in the locality. I have no knowledge of how they felt about the house when they saw what they had created. I trust that after so much trouble and expense they were pleased with the result. In any case they were now housed, if not with elegance or convenience at least, on a scale which seemed to them suitable. The charms of the interior I will describe in a moment.

My grandfather died in 1884, but for ten years or more before that event my father had been living contentedly at Hinton, after a few years in the Rifle Brigade, perfectly happy to spend his life quietly in the country with his hunting and his shooting. I have the impression that he had no intention of marrying, and looked to his younger brother to carry on the line—a purpose which in those days was considered important. Unluckily, however, his brother died in 1886 and my father, then just on 40, felt he should search for a bride. A year later he became engaged to my mother, Blanche Cave, who was exactly half his age.

When making his proposal he had said: 'Will you make this house your home', thus modestly offering the house rather than himself. Had my mother been sensitive to architecture she might well have replied: 'I will take you, but I can't face the house.' However, this impasse did not arise, and after a token period of reflection she accepted the offer which I think she had been for some time eagerly awaiting.

For the first few years of her marriage my mother kept a rather sketchy diary. At the beginning all was excitement. To find herself the mistress of a large country house instead of just one daughter in a family of five children, and never on the easiest terms with her mother, was an exciting experience. The pages of the visitors' book for the summer of 1888 were filled with the names of her relations who had come to stay and see how happily little Blanche was settled.

But gradually the tone changed, and there were constant references to 'this barracks of a house', for she was obviously beginning to find that life was far from easy in this exceedingly ill-designed building. She came from a wealthy family, and her father had inherited about a million on the death of his miserly father. Ever since this event shortage of money was unknown in her family. But this had not been so before this welcome death: her parents had been so poorly provided for that they had left England to live in Florence, like a number of other impoverished English. There my mother was born, and did not come to England until she was three years old. But in the '80s all this was happily changed, and there was the large country house which her father had built at Ditcham near Petersfield, a house in Lowndes Square, and a steam yacht of considerable size. At Hinton the situation was sadly different.

When my grandfather had rebuilt Hinton agricultural prosperity was at its height, and since his income came principally from land he had been rather well-off. No doubt he had spent a part of his available capital on the house, and then on the church, and a little later on providing an entirely new church on his property at Kingsley, near Alton. All this left his income from land intact, and there was no reason to suppose that there would be any change in the future. About 1875, however, the prosperity which agriculture had enjoyed for a number of years past suddenly collapsed, and this national industry, on which a large section of the community depended, ceased to provide both employment and support. The cause of the disaster was the importation of large quantities of foreign wheat, chiefly from the new corn-growing areas of America where costs were low. The English market was thus flooded with cheap corn; and at the same time, by an unfortunate chance, English farmers suffered a succession of three ruined harvests. Few farmers had any capital to fall back on, and they were thus unable to carry on.

In these circumstances farm rents fell heavily, and farms which had become vacant were almost unlettable and sometimes were left derelict. My father, I know, had to take over one or two farms in addition to the home farm since tenants were not to be found. At the time of his marriage in 1888 my father's financial position was still very indifferent, and he certainly hoped that a bride from an affluent family would improve his situation. But in this he was rather disappointed, for my mother was given only half of what her elder sister had received on marriage, the remainder not following until her father's death. In fact I think my maternal grandfather had found that he was dissipating his large inheritance rather too quickly. Like my paternal grandfather he was an enthusiastic builder, and had erected not only the house at Ditcham but also a Catholic church and priest's house in Petersfield; for he and my grandmother had been received into the Roman Catholic Church in 1882 under the guidance of Father (later Cardinal) Gasquet, a devoted friend.

Thus my parents' early married life at Hinton was distinctly threadbare, and my unfortunate mother found herself called upon to deal with a situation which was entirely new to her. Servants, it is true, were usually available and wages were disgracefully low, but already they were to some degree able to choose places where life was fairly comfortable and pleasant, and Hinton can hardly have been one of those.

In 1892 my father's financial position was materially improved by the death of his uncle, Ralph Dutton, when the entailed properties of Timsbury and Bedhampton came into his possession, while in the last year of the century my maternal grandfather died and my mother inherited the second half of the dowry that had been hoped for on her marriage. Thus when I first became conscious of my surroundings, there had already been a softening of the austere conditions which had prevailed at Hinton in the nineteenth century. The way of life and the domestic discomforts seem so remote in these days that they are perhaps worth describing.

My grandfather's injunction that there was to be no bathroom in the house was faithfully carried out, and as my father had a dislike of change which amounted to a phobia, the house remained without this almost essential convenience until 1919. As planned, however, there were four W.C.s, one above the other for convenience of drainage, with a fifth in the wing for the maids. For the period this was perhaps an adequate supply, but unfortunately owing to a miscalculation on the part of the builder only two out of the four superimposed 'Loos' functioned. The one in the cellar, designed I suppose for the use of the men-servants, was found to lie below the level of the drains and so was quite useless, and indeed was quickly done away with; that on the second floor on the other hand was above the level of the water supply and so was almost equally unsatisfactory. While my parents were childless—as they were for the first six years of marriage—the bedrooms on the second floor were not used so that it was immaterial whether the W.C. functioned or not, but when there were nurseries on that floor something had to be done. There was no water pressure for the usual 'pull-up' contraption, but eventually a low-level cistern was devised into which water entered very slowly so that the plug could only be pulled at long intervals. It was, at least, better than nothing.

The water for the W.C.s came from a tank filled by rain-water from the roof. In a dry spell the tank of course emptied very quickly and when this was found to be the case it could be filled, with great labour, by a hand pump from another rain-water tank beneath the terrace. In wet weather all sorts of curious things were swept off the roof into the tanks and so found their way into the W.C.s, thus greatly adding to their interest, but unfortunately frequently blocking the pipes. The intention of this unsatisfactory use of rain-water was to lessen the amount of water pumped from the old well in the orchard, the well, as I have already mentioned, which had lain under the floor of the kitchen in the Tudor house. From this well the water was raised to inadequate tanks in the roof of the house by a pump worked by a superannuated carriage horse. Every morning this elderly Dobbin was led off to his dreary task of walking round and round on a narrow path dragging the beam of the pump. Once started he would continue till he was stopped, so that no superintendence was required. It was anyhow quite an easy and undemanding employment.

Thus, although rather precarious, a water-supply to the house existed; but naturally there was no electricity supply, and lighting depended on lamps and candles. In country houses electric light was not very usual until the first years of this century, and at Hinton, which was hardly *avant-garde*, there was no supply till 1913. An engine was then installed which produced a dim 50 volt light.

The house was, however, built with a very restricted system of central heating. This consisted of two coils of very large pipes, one in the entrance hall and one in the north end of the drawing-room. Both were encased in cast iron cages with white marble tops. The water was heated by a small boiler in the cellar, which required stoking every few hours. This was the job of the footman, and thunderous echoes from the pipes indicated that he was busy at his subterranean task.

When I was a small boy the decoration of the house still remained much as when it was built, and I remember the gloomy aspect of the rooms fairly clearly. The entrance hall, which faced north, was anyhow rather dark, and its sombre appearance was not helped by the fact that the windows were filled with opaque glass. This had been an idea of my grandmother's, so that, when visitors called, she could escape from the drawing-room to the staircase at the other end of the hall without being observed by those in the carriage at the front door. It was a practical notion, but not one designed to add to the gaiety of the room.

The window glass was not the only sobering feature of the hall. There was a heavy varnished oak chimney-piece, surmounted by the family arms and the doors were in the same material with coarse mouldings, which would have been better forgotten, picked out in shining black paint. Lincrusta, in shades of dark green and cream, was freely used for a dado up to the uncomfortable height of 4½ feet, for a deep frieze, and on the ceiling where panels of it were set between plaster ribs painted to imitate oak.

The walls between the dado and the frieze were naturally not left to themselves but were covered with an assortment of objects supposed presumably to have ornamental value. There were sundry antlers and horns, a pair of alarming looking long-muzzled guns and a number of pistols. Amongst these trophies were prints and a few oil paintings of horses which intimated to a visitor that he was entering a sporting rather than an aesthetic house. There was also a quantity of furniture, of which a large writing table was the most solid piece arranged for two writers, who would dip their pens into bronze inkstands fashioned as dogs' heads.

Opening out of the hall at the east end was the drawing-room which had fulfilled my grandmother's stipulation for a spacious room. It was in two parts, an anteroom, with a wide opening into the southern or main section. This was lit by a large bow window to the south and other windows to the east. Early photographs show the room rather sparsely furnished, and perhaps the agricultural depression had begun to set in before it was properly filled with bric-à-brac. The furniture from the previous drawing-room would anyhow have been inadequate to fill the new room. The curtains, however, were rather lavish in canary yellow and Prussian blue, with deep silk pelmets hung from gilt cornices and edged with silk-covered wooden 'bobbles'. In the 'greenery yallery' period of the '90s my mother found these brilliantly contrasting colours offensive, and she had the wide blue velvet borders removed, but fortunately kept the material, and this was put back again half a century later when Victoriana came into fashion once again.

Suitable pictures to cover the spacious bare walls were obviously a problem, as there were not nearly enough family portraits to make an effect. This was partly remedied by having copies made of portraits from both sides of the family and these, when set in heavy gilt frames, created an imposing effect. But the largest picture was a life-sized group of my father with his brother and sister as children painted about 1860. The artist was Edwin Long, who later was to gain a great reputation for his vast subject pictures, but who is now quite rightly forgotten. His most famous picture was 'The Marriage Market'—a very different subject to the prim little Duttons—which was bought by Mr. Holloway for £7,000 and now hangs in the gallery at the Royal Holloway College, that remarkable building at Esher which emulates and excels in size the Château de Chambord in Touraine.

The ornaments consisted of a large quantity of china, for my grandmother was an eager, if undiscriminating, collector. An inelegant glass-fronted cabinet of Dutch manufacture contained a part of the collection, and the remainder was displayed on tables and on clumsy gilt side tables backed with mirrors. Nothing was of any merit, and the value of the whole contents of the room would be very small.

The adjacent library calls for no particular remark. There were bookshelves on the walls filled with a fine selection of sermons, a heavy chimney-piece of brawn-like marble, and dark green rep curtains. In the dining-room the curtains were of the same material but crimson in colour and a Turkey carpet covered the floor. On the walls were two large nineteenth-century seascapes of little ships being tossed about on angry yellow seas. They were not at all the sort of pictures to study during meals. The furniture was rather sensational, and consisted of an extensive suite emanating, I would say, from the Low Countries. It was made in some cheap wood but stained almost black to imitate old oak and was elaborately carved. The largest piece was the sideboard in which a pair of 'sedent' lions holding shields supported the board, above which rose a great expanse of mirror set in a carved frame. As a small child I enjoyed crawling about amongst the lions but quite early it dawned on me that this was one of the ugliest pieces of furniture ever created.

From the service door of the dining-room a long stone-flagged passage stretched away to the distant kitchen, passing *en route* the pantry, the butler's bedroom, the housekeeper's room and the still room on the north side, and the back stairs, the brushing room (where the footman slept) and a dismal little room known as the smoking-room on the south side. The latter had been broadmindedly provided by my grandfather for the use of my father and his friends, and having a door into the garden the unpleasant vapours could easily be expelled. In later years, when its use as a smoking-room had long since vanished, it was called instead the gun-room, though I do not remember ever seeing a gun in it.

The kitchen, I think, was the creation of my grandfather. It extended upwards for the whole three floors of the house, 35 or 40 feet, I suppose; this extraordinary height being intended to keep it reasonably airy. This would have been more effective if the builder, with his complete disregard for aspect, had not placed it on the south side of the house, but even so some of the heat from the impressive range of stoves no doubt found its way into the upper regions. The stoves were divided into three sections: in the middle was the usual type of huge range, on the left of it was a contraption designed for cooking with charcoal, and on the right a very large hot-plate. Neither of these two latter was ever used in my conscious lifetime.

Elaborate cooking arrangements were necessary when one considers the number of meals the cook and her two assistants were expected to produce every day. There were meals for the dining-room, for the schoolroom, for the nursery, for the housekeeper's room, and for the servants' hall; and all this in a house run on austere economical lines. Certainly the schoolroom and the nursery did not exist for very long as separate entities, and no doubt the housekeeper's room and the servants' hall were only individual for some meals. Nevertheless the work must have been enormous.

When I altered the house in 1936 and the floor of the kitchen was taken up it was found that the stone flags were precariously lodged over a fairly deep well. Fortunately this happened to be in the middle of the room, and so under the massive kitchen table. Had it been otherwise the cook might at any time have disappeared suddenly into the underworld.

There were also, of course, larders and a big scullery with a bread-oven in one corner, and round these offices the kitchen passage wound desperately towards the back door, at times dimly lit, at others plunged into inky darkness. At the end of the north-ward pointing branch of the wing was the servants' hall, and from this a staircase ascended to three bedrooms for visiting men-servants, cunningly planned so that intercourse with the resident maids would have entailed a long and hazardous journey.

The whole service wing in fact was designed on a scale quite out of proportion to the polite part of the house which was relatively small. Possibly this disproportion was usual in houses of that date, but I would suppose that my grandparents being used to a really big house were inclined to think that all this extensive paraphernalia was essential.

The first floor followed the lines of the ground floor. In the main part of the house were a number of spare bedrooms, and in the middle facing south my parents' bedroom, a dressing-room, and my mother's sitting-room over the dining-room. When my father's younger brother had died in 1884 his furniture and effects had been put into this latter room, and my mother had taken it over just as it was; and thus it remained for the 48 years she lived at Hinton. She introduced her books of which she had many, and a table covered with plants in the window, but these were almost the only additions. Although she had a rather vivid personality, she in no way imparted this to her surroundings.

Away from the main part of the house a bleak, institutional passage stretched away to the maids' quarters. The builder with his usual obtuseness had placed the back stairs and windows lighting the passage on the south side, so that here were only two sunny rooms, while those on the north received no ray of sunshine.

The two south rooms were the schoolroom and the governess's bedroom. The former was one of the few agreeable rooms in the house, for my mother, as her brood increased, added a bow-window which, unlike other windows in the house, which were either too high in the room, or too low, or in one corner, lighted the room admirably. It contained the usual sort of schoolroom furniture, a large oak table in the middle with a green leather top on which we did our lessons seated on robust Victorian mahogany chairs; against one wall was a cottage piano on which my sisters hammered out their scales and little pieces. It was early decided, apparently, that I was not a musical type, and no time was wasted on tuition in this direction. A bookcase contained the lesson books, and a little simple reading in French and German—*Les Malheurs de Sophie* and so forth—while for entertainment there were a number of books of fairy stories—Hans Andersen, very sentimental, Grimm, frightening, and Andrew Lang, a varied selection. In the window was an ottoman for repose above and with a useful receptacle for oddments below, but I remember no pictures on the flowered wallpaper, nor indeed any single object of any beauty in the room which could have inspired the youthful mind.

In the little adjacent room the sequence of four German governesses who superintended the education of my two elder sisters, and myself before I went to school, spent many hours of their dreary lives. These ladies were Fräulein von Brandt, Mehrendorf, Bömark and Wedekind. I think I got on quite well with all of them, even Fräulein Mehrendorf, a formidable, moustached figure, but Fräulien Wedekind was the only one for whom I had any affection.

Victorian Comfort and Beauty

The first and the last were unfortunately suffering from affairs of the heart while they were at Hinton. Fräulein von Brandt, who was young and pretty, had become engaged to the son of her former employer, a German princeling, and had been sent over to England to get her out of the way. Angelika Wedekind was passionately in love with, and thought she was engaged to, a Herr von Schöning in her home town of Altona. We knew his appearance well from a photograph, a rather flashy-looking man with an upturned moustache like the Kaiser. There were tears in the schoolroom when no letter came as expected, and we children were begged to pray in church that Monday morning would remedy the situation. But I fear our prayers were not generally efficacious.

One day, however, a very disturbing letter arrived saying that Herr von Schöning was in financial difficulties and could his Angelika help him. Several days of intense *Sturm und Drang* followed, and we children proffered useful advice. Eventually Fräulein Wedekind sent off to Altona what must have been the greater part of her small savings. Thereafter the letters became fewer than ever, until they ceased altogether. Herr von Schöning, I very much fear, was an adventurer.

While these dramas were being enacted on the south side of the passage, all was peace and quiet in my father's rooms on the north, so long as he was left to himself. My parents, economical in all else, were prodigal in their use of rooms; and indeed why not? There were plenty. Between them they had a bedroom, two dressing-rooms, two sitting-rooms, and my father's carpentering-room.

The first room along the passage was his sitting-room, which had considerable character, in fact was the only room in the house which had any character at all. The walls were closely covered with pictures, many being Bartolozzi prints representing mythological subjects, which here made their rather unexpected appearance. Possibly they had belonged to his mother. More in keeping with my father's interests were a number of agreeable aquatints of famous horses; but dominating all else were three large oil paintings of his favourite dogs.

These needless to say had been painted before he had been burdened with a family, but all through his life he very sensibly greatly preferred his dogs to his children. The former gave him undemanding companionship and devotion, the latter seldom provided these comforts. The central picture of the three represented a brown and white spaniel, John Rover, whose bones had already been resting for several years in a quiet corner of the garden when I was born. He was painted life size and full length— horizontally, of course, like Sir Brooke Boothby in Wright of Derby's portrait in the Tate Gallery—and stories of his intelligence still lived. My father would tell us that when he came in from shooting John Rover would scamper upstairs and come down with his slippers in his mouth. Possibly this story contained a hint for his children, but if so I fear it was a hint never taken.

There was much else in the room. The panels of the door had been painted by my father's sister, my Aunt Louisa, with scenes of kingfishers flying amongst reeds, and she had also worked a brightly coloured cushion for the window-seat. Over the chimney-piece was an overmantel made up of panels carved by my father. On the left of the chimney-breast was a bookcase containing the books one would expect. Surtees and Whyte-Melville, books on shooting, hunting and pugilism interspersed with a number of late Victorian and Edwardian autobiographies. On the table by my father's chair there was generally to be seen one of Marie Corelli's uplifting novels. Behind the chair was a glass-fronted case containing his most prized possessions—his guns. These were never trusted in the gun-room but were kept here under his eye where they could be oiled, polished and generally fondled.

There was a good deal of furniture, but it was particularly the writing table which used to interest me when I was young since it was loaded with little gadgets for which my father had a great weakness. There were a number of knives for trimming his quill pens, a stamp for dating letters, an address stamp for insignificant correspondence, a mechanical contrivance for sharpening pencils, a variety of little machines for clipping together papers, and all the other appurtenances of a Victorian desk. The use of all these labour-saving contrivances occupied a great deal of his time.

Next door to the sitting-room was the carpentering-room, in which my father spent many happy hours. He was remarkably deft with his fingers, and when younger had embellished with carving many otherwise harmless pieces of furniture. The last of his rooms was his dressing-room. It was strangely placed, as far as could be from his bedroom; but his father had used it as such, ostensibly in order to keep an eye on the maids whose bedrooms lay beyond the baize door, and so he continued the inconvenient arrangement.

On the top floor, in the rooms which filled the area of the Georgian house, were the nurseries, which later became the bedrooms for my three sisters and myself. In one of the north-facing rooms was the fire-escape which was an object of great childish interest. It consisted of a thick canvas chute attached at the top to an iron frame hinged to the window-sill. When required for use, it was simply tipped up and the tube fell outside to the ground where the hammock-like end could be held out to receive those descending. It was a practical contraption down which a child could be sent with safety.

Every few months we would have an exercise. Men-servants and gardeners would be assembled below to hold the hammock, and we would be at the top awaiting our turn to descend. There was a rope in the tube, but the secret of making an easy descent was to press outwards with bottom and knees and so regulate the speed of descent. To give us confidence my mother would go first. Wrapping her long skirts round her ankles she would descend with great poise and arrive unruffled in the hammock on ground level. Then we children would go down rather enjoying the excitement and sometimes having a second shot. Lastly it was the turn of the nurserymaid; the nurse would never attempt it and apparently would have preferred to burn to death.

Although the nurserymaids changed, the performance was always the same. Almost fainting with alarm, as if being taken to the scaffold, she would somehow be coerced on to the window-sill with her feet in the mouth of the terrible monster whose gullet opened below her, and too terrified to move. Eventually, probably pushed by the nurse, she would slip over the brink but clinging for dear life to the rope would stick a yard or two down. From ground level, where we awaited her arrival, the canvas tube looked like a snake which had swallowed too large a rabbit. At last exhorted from below the poor girl would leave go of the rope and forgetting all injunction about bottom and knees would shoot down to arrive in the hammock in a state of complete disarray with her skirt over her head, greatly to the amusement and delight of the men assembled below.

From the nursery landing a short passage led eastwards up some steps to two large attics which covered the area of the drawing room on the ground floor. Although, when I was young, the house had been in existence for only about 40 years the amount of lumber which had here accumulated was remarkable. These large rooms were both crowded with it. There was furniture, pictures, books, stuffed birds in glass cases, portfolios containing an assortment of prints and drawings, the debris of discarded amusements, broken croquet mallets, the paraphernalia of toxophily, a box of mahogany bowls, and everywhere evidence of my grandmother's passion for collecting china, huge Dresden ornaments, figures, candlesticks, dinner and dessert services and much else.

An object which greatly interested me was my grandfather's shower-bath. This consisted of a small circular tank raised on 6-foot supports with a pan below. The tank was presumably filled with water of a suitable temperature by a footman standing on a chair; my grandfather then stepped into the pan, pulled a string, and down came the very transitory shower. Another form of bath which had found its way into the lumber-room was my father's Turkish bath. This was a wooden box which would be set up in his dressing-room; he would sit inside it with only his head and hands emerging through holes as if in the pillory, while an oil lamp at the side puffed hot air into the box. I think it must have been rather soon discarded. Another aid to health and beauty was a back-board. It was an austere contraption covered in green baize with a depression for the back of the head. It could be propped up at an angle of 30° from the floor, and there the victims would lie as long as was bearable. It had been contrived for my Aunt Louisa, who was born with a twisted spine, but I fear that in her case it failed in its objective.

I have often wished that when I came to disperse this extraordinary collection in 1936 that I had had a wider knowledge as amongst the assemblage of junk there may well have been some objects of value. Some things I did save, amongst them some handsome late seventeenth-century oak balustrading, which had somehow made its appearance here. This now slightly altered serves very happily as altar rails in the church.

On the west side of the central block a sinister passage wound away through the top floor of the wing. Starting fairly normally with a few maids' bedrooms it then abandoned all attempt at sanity and disintegrated into extraordinary dark corners, box-rooms, cupboards, tanks, trap-doors into the roof, and so forth. In one dark corner stood my mother's trousseau trunk, a huge black affair lined with linen and with her new initials, B.D., painted in red on its arched lid. One wonders whether the high hopes with which this trunk must have been packed were fulfilled. It seems astonishing that anyone could have seriously designed anything so impracticable as this passage: for children's games of hide and seek, however, it was perfect.

This, then, was the house into which my mother had married and which, in spite of heroic efforts, remained little changed when she left it almost half a century later. My father's rigid objection to any alteration made improvement almost impossible, and had he been left to himself, he would have allowed the house to fall about him rather than do anything to repair it. This is not an unusual complex: there are a number of country houses about England—some of architectural interest—where the owners see ruin descending without making the smallest effort to retard it. In the case of the Victorian Hinton this would not have been of great moment.

Georgian Revival

Anyone who has been patient enough to read through the foregoing long description of the Victorian Hinton, will gather that it was not a building which was particularly sympathetic to me, and it is not surprising that for a number of years before my father's death I had been considering how I could convert it into a house which I would find agreeable. I naturally made no mention of this intention to my father who would I fear have been horrified both at the idea of altering the structure and also at the capital, which he had carefully accumulated, being used for this purpose. For a number of years after the transformation had taken place I would have a dream, it amounted I think to a nightmare, that my father had somehow come to life again and that I was under the necessity of explaining to him what had occurred.

My grandfather had clearly been an enthusiastic builder and no doubt my love for bricks and mortar was inherited from him, although our tastes were very different—and who shall say which was the better. At least, however, I had a clearer conception of planning. My father lived to a ripe age: when he died in January 1935 he was within a few days of his 88th birthday. I was 36, which is quite a satisfactory age for starting on a building project of some size; the basic lines of my plans had had time to mature. I was not sorry, it must be owned, to have adequate excuse for making radical alterations at Hinton, for, though I loved the place, the atmosphere of the house was not to me a happy one. I could reverse what Edward Gibbon had written of Buriton and to say that during my youth I had there passed 'some light and many heavy hours'.

My general intention was to uncover the central Georgian block with its five south windows, build an entirely new block on the west side of it with a dining-room facing south, and give the whole an eighteenth-century appearance with Georgian sash-windows and a parapet above the first floor with the second floor in a Mansard roof. The north-pointing foot of the 'L'-shaped wing was to be cut off, the second floor eliminated, and a parapet as on the main block to be carried round, where the gables had been, with a low mansard behind it. The windows, however, were to be left as a memento of the Victorian phase. This was a mistake, I think, as they are very ugly.

With this broad outline sketched out, I put the enterprise into the capable hands of Lord Gerald Wellesley and Mr. Trenwith Wills, who were in partnership as architects. The planning of the main block was fairly simple for most of the existing walls were to be retained. Indeed on the ground floor, apart from the building of a new dining-room, the only alteration was to move the dividing wall between the library and the existing dining-room, so that the former was lighted by three windows and the room adjoining, which became my sitting-room, by two. This, I think, must have been the original arrangement. The drawing-room was to be given a swelling, semicircular bay-window in place of the battlemented Victorian monstrosity, and the new dining-room was similarly treated so that the main block was completely symmetrical. On the first floor there was to be a generous supply of bathrooms—I had too long suffered from a scarcity—and this by the suppression of a few small rooms was easily achieved, so that there were seven principal bedrooms and six bathrooms.

The planning of the main block was fairly straightforward, but the service wing was more complex. Not only was the wing smaller, but also the domestic arrangements had to be planned for a way of life quite different and far more restricted than had been en-visaged in my grandfather's day. All this, and a mass of detail took many months of anxious thought and discussion to prepare, but eventually the plans and elevations were finalized, and seemed to me very satisfactory. I could hardly believe I was to live in a house I could look at without pain.

The rather long delay, in fact, was of no consequence, for obviously it would be impossible to live in the house during this drastic transformation, and we, as a family, had to be accommo-dated elsewhere. My mother was the first to leave Hinton in the early summer of 1936. With admirable forethought my father had bought for her some years before his death a charming small Queen Anne house, Bramdean Manor, which adjoined the Hinton property. Thither she went, as soon as some alterations had been made, with the utmost joy and relief. At last she had a small house which was truly her own and to which she could do as she wished. She passed the remaining 11 years of her life there in great happiness. The rest of the family dispersed soon after, my sisters to various homes of their own, and I going to Bedhampton Manor, an agreeable old house in a not very agreeable locality near Havant, which I had inherited from my father and which happened to be vacant. As with my mother, this was the first occasion on which I had lived in a house in the country which seemed really my own, and my pleasure and contentment were unbounded. Thus by July 1936 the poor Victorian building at Hinton was standing grim and desolate awaiting the arrival of the housebreakers. It had been in existence for just on 70 years.

This was the only moment, I think, that I had any qualms about the operation I had put into train. Many people had counselled prudence and waiting for a few years until my financial position was clearer; for death duties were not yet finally assessed, let alone paid, owing to the extraordinary dilatoriness of my father's solicitor. Only in the following year did it become apparent that this dilatoriness concealed fraudulence, and the fact that he was sent to prison for seven years provided no financial compensation for the large sums he had made away with. But had I delayed starting work, the war would have been upon us, the house as it stood would have been an obvious candidate for military occupation, and who knows what could have been done with it when the war ended.

Fortunately, however, I was still young enough to take no notice of sensible advice, and so the work proceeded. Before the end of July 1936 the forecourt was filled with the contractor's tackle and impedimenta. Two wooden huts had been set up, one for the contractor's foreman, the other for the clerk of the works, an admirable man who represented my interests. Between these two adjacent buildings a sort of Montagu and Capulet relationship persisted throughout the building operations.

Perhaps in order to make a good show at once, the contractor started by demolishing the northward end of the service wing. This, in fact, was an error. A reader who has had the patience to follow the previous chapter may remember that at the end of the bottom stroke of the 'L' there was a large servants' hall from which a staircase led up to three bedrooms on the two floors above. Had this end of the wing been temporarily left as an isolated tower, it would have afforded admirable accommodation for workmen. For accommodation was a major difficulty. Nowadays workmen have cars and can live or lodge anywhere within a radius of 10 miles or so of the site. In 1936 it was necessary to find beds in the close vicinity, and this was almost impossible. In the event those workmen who could find nothing better simply dossed down in the harness-room of the stables, where the conditions were such that they would have caused anxiety to the local Health Officer had he seen them.

After the demolition of the end of the wing, the next step was to break a gap right through the house on the west side of the original Georgian block to form a space for the new dining-room on the south side, and lavatories, a pantry and a stair on the north. The house thus temporarily in two parts had a very strange appearance, and those seeing it would say 'this looks like something from the Spanish Civil War'. Little did we then think that shortly we should have equally good similes from much nearer home.

Thus the work proceeded through the months, the straightforward lines of the neo-Georgian building gradually emerging through the Victorian Tudor as crockets, gables and battlements gave way to a brick parapet, and the plate glass and heavy stone mouldings of the windows were replaced by small paned sashes with wooden astrigals. Soon the angular and clumsy bows were torn down and serene, swelling bays began to rise on the drawing-room and new dining-room block. I had hoped that the south front of the Georgian block would have survived, but we found that once the nineteenth-century bow had been demolished and the windows altered there would have been almost nothing left of it, so this section was rebuilt from cellar level. In other parts much of the Victorian brickwork remained, and this when given natural coloured pointing, was quite pleasant in effect. Furthermore the stone quoins, which had weathered to an agreeable grey, were kept wherever possible, and the stone Gothic moulding which surrounded the main block was shaved flat, and so made an effective little feature below the first-floor windows.

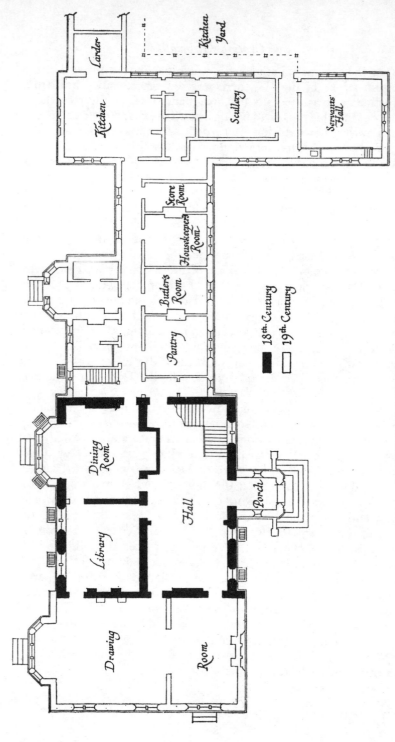

GROUND FLOOR PLAN, before alteration

Larder

Kitchen Yard

Kitchen

Scullery

Servants' Hall

Store Room

Housekeepers Room

Butler's Room

Pantry

18th Century

19th Century

Dining Room

Library

Hall

Porch

Drawing

Room

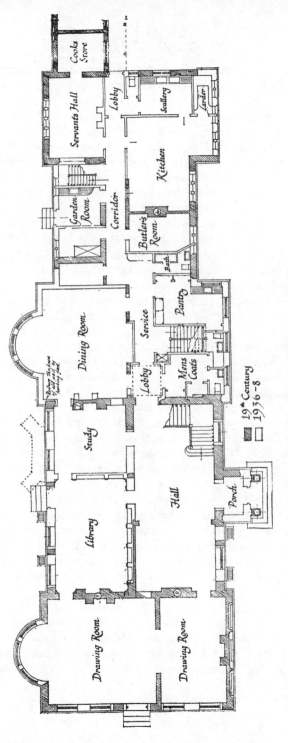

GROUND FLOOR PLAN, as altered

Cooks Store

Servants Hall

Lobby

Scullery

Larder

Garden Room

Corridor

Kitchen

Butler's Room

Bath

Dining Room

Service

Pantry

Below Harbour if old wall by Partridge front

Lobby

Study

Mens Coats

■ 19th Century
□ 1936-8

Library

Hall

Drawing Room

Porch

Drawing Room

Meanwhile I was scouring the country for internal features which could be incorporated in the new building. As it happened Robert Adam's Adelphi Terrace in London was to be demolished in 1937: a major crime in my opinion, but one from which I benefited considerably. A sale of fittings was held on the site, and bidding energetically I obtained a number of doors and architraves, carved window-shutters, and several chimney-pieces, two of which of simple Adam design in white marble were for the new dining-room and my own sitting-room. Soon after, in this iconoclastic year, Norfolk House in St. James's Square was also torn down, and here I bought many square yards of wide oak boards, and an attractive steel grate similar to the one in the Norfolk room in the Victoria and Albert Museum. This fitted well into a majestic Porphyry chimney-piece, originally at Hamilton Palace, which I had bought for the entrance hall.

Porphyry chimney-pieces are fairly rare, and I was delighted to hear from Lord Gerald Wellesley that he had heard of another. We went to see it at Staines where it was lying dismantled in a shed. It was a handsome Empire affair with good ormolu mounts, and obviously right in period for the Library which was to have a Regency aspect. The significance of the ormolu plaque in the frieze puzzled me for a long time. There were many figures but what exactly they were doing I could not determine. Some years later, however, going round the Vatican Gallery I went into a small room and there before me was the original fresco of my plaque. It was '*Le Nozze Aldobrandine*', which dated from the Augustan age. It had been discovered on the Esquiline in 1605, and was removed to its present place in 1838. In the early nineteenth century it became a popular subject and was repeated in many forms. The group of female figures on the left-hand side were apparently giving last counsels and encouragement to the bride for the ordeal which lay before her, while the disconsolate male figure sitting on the edge of the bed was presumably the young husband. The scene did not suggest that a very happy night was in store.

The incorporation of the Adelphi woodwork undoubtedly delayed progress, and provided a valid excuse to the contractor for what seemed to me a slow advance. However, in view of the great amount of work which had to be done, I think I may have been rather impatient. But in the spring of 1938, seeing no chance of the house being finished for many months, I asked the contractor to concentrate on the service wing, so that I could return there while the main part of the house was still incomplete. Thus about midsummer of 1938 I was able to move into Hinton although the main rooms were still without floors or plaster.

As the summer advanced the threat of war became increasingly acute, and already the contractor was finding it difficult to obtain various materials, such as copper for the flat of the roof. The outlook became more and more grim, and I began to envisage being left with the empty shell of the house. No one, I feel bound to admit, could have welcomed the respite of the Munich agreement with greater warmth. With this national breather arranged, work continued on the house throughout the winter. I had decided that no decorations were to be done for six months after the work was completed in order to let the plaster on the walls dry thoroughly—quick-drying plaster was seemingly not then in use— but as it transpired it was more than six years before the rooms were painted.

The first room to become habitable in the main part of the house was the dining-room, and in the course of the winter I was able to use it as a sitting-room, a most welcome expansion, and since the service door opened into the kitchen passage there was no necessity to go through the unfinished entrance hall. Maintaining a constant pressure the last workman was squeezed out of the house in the early summer of 1939, and, although the bare plaster walls were not very handsome, I was able to get my furniture out of store, put carpets down and curtains up, so that the house had a reasonable appearance.

Concentrating on my own interests, I was taking, I fear, little notice of international affairs. In the course of the summer I had been given the choice in the event of war of accommodating 40 children evacuated from London or of giving the house over to the Portsmouth Day School for Girls. The latter seemed the only possible of the two alternatives, but even the arrival of 100 camp-beds and various other impedimenta, which were stored in the cellars, failed to make the threat of war seem very serious.

Towards the middle of August the small staff I had gathered went off on their summer holidays and I too left Hinton. The situation, even I had to admit, was looking very bad; but it came as a shock to receive a telegram on 29th August to say that the school had been ordered to move into Hinton 48 hours later. I rushed home, and the following day, with the aid of employees and removal men from Winchester, we desperately cleared the house as far as possible of the furniture and carpets which I had lately arranged with so much joy. The Library, it had been agreed, should be kept for storage, and all that could not be piled into it was stacked in the harness-room of the stables. On the last day of the month the house was as clear of its more valuable contents as it could be made in so short a time; and I awaited invasion.

Punctually at 10 o'clock in the morning a fleet of buses drew up at the front door, out poured a crowd of little girls, each carrying a small suitcase, and came shouting and laughing into the house, up and down stairs and into all the rooms. It was a real St. Trinian's scene. But for me it was a moment of intense bitterness: just as the many months of work and effort had reached their culmination, all was snatched from me. Nowadays one is more accustomed to the buffets of fortune, but in 1939 I found it difficult to comprehend that I was being turned out of my own house. However, the situation had to be accepted, and picking up my suitcase, I left.

Within a few days I was fortunate enough to get a very humble job in the Foreign Office, and there I remained for 69 months neither rising nor falling in my status—indeed the latter would have been difficult. The break with my former life was sudden and complete. It resembled having a plaster pulled sharply off one's stomach, the pain was intense but not prolonged. While many of my friends were still floundering and wondering what to do with their lives and their houses, I was already modestly incorporated into the war machine. The department, of which I was a doubtful ornament, worked all round the clock, and although night duty was detestable there was for me a particular compensation in that the rota was so arranged that we had two completely free days in sixteen. Thus I was able to go to the country and, staying with my mother, keep an eye on the happenings at Hinton. As the war advanced, and I heard of the fate of many country houses in military occupation, I realized how fortunate I was to have my house populated by little girls, although they were hardly angels. I was glad, too, that no decorations had been carried out, so that there was not very much to spoil. In any case there was no doubt that the house was admirably adapted to use as a school.

A couple of months before the outbreak of war, I had agreed, at Lord Gerald Wellesley's instigation, to erect in the dining-room a plaster ceiling designed by Robert Adam, which was about to be destroyed in the demolition of 37 Berkeley Square. This had been Lord Rosebery's house, and in the nineteenth century a singularly ugly scarlet brick façade had been constructed across two eighteenth-century houses, thus giving them the appearance of a single building. The ceiling, of a typically graceful Adam design, was embellished with a number of roundels painted by Angelica Kauffmann, or one of her school. These being on thick paper were detachable. For the plaster itself it was necessary to take a model—a squeeze as it is professionally called—of one-quarter of the ceiling; the whole could then be reproduced in fibrous plaster, and the original demolished. This then was the programme.

In the ensuing turmoil I had forgotten all about this project, but to my surprise in the summer of 1940 I heard from the contractors that the ceiling was ready to be put up and that either this must be done or it would have to be destroyed, as they could not keep it. Since I was given the alternatives, I naturally decided on the former, and during August, when the children of the school had dispersed for holidays, several able-bodied men came down to Hinton and carried out this wholly unnecessary work. It was sadly indicative of lack of organization at that dark period of the war, when invasion seemed far from improbable, that these men could not have been put to more useful work. However, the job was done, and looked very well, although, of course, the decoration was left for a future date.

Slowly and monotonously the years passed, and by the early spring of 1945 it was clear that the war in Europe was in its last phase. I therefore learnt without great surprise, but with intense joy, that the school would not be returning to Hinton after the Easter holidays, and that the house would once more be in my possession. But, alas, my joy was of the shortest. Early in April my agent received a letter saying that a party from the Service Departments and headed by the Astronomer Royal would be coming to Hinton on 16th April to inspect it with a view to compulsorily acquiring it as the new Royal Observatory.

One had little resilience at that time and I was cast into utter despair. What could I do? The Service Departments had complete autocratic power: the engagement of Crichel Down at which their tyranny was finally defeated was far in the future. The only opposition I could muster was to meet the party and give vent to my feelings. Therefore, getting leave from the Office, where my work had been by no means receiving my full attention for several days, I was on the doorstep of Hinton when the party of 20 or so arrived.

No host could have had more unwelcome guests, and no guests, as I could easily perceive, had less pleasure in seeing their host. They had not expected that the owner would be present. I led the way into the house, and made what was, I fear, a very emotional oration saying that my family had lived in the place for three and a half centuries and that I would sooner lose an arm or a leg than lose the house, and much else. The party looked acutely embarrassed, not for themselves but for me who was making such an hysterical exhibition; and indeed with the house in its then condition, with paraphernalia of the school in all the rooms, it must have seemed eccentric to feel so strongly about retaining it.

When my little speech was ended the party dispersed to examine the house and garden, while electric machines whirled away in the forecourt testing I know not what. The Astronomer Royal, Sir Harold Spencer Jones, took me aside and spoke kindly to me, but made it apparent that he was not deviating in any way from his nefarious project. After three hours the party withdrew, politely thanking me for their visit. I was not able to return the compliment. After ten days of terrible anxiety my agent received a note from the Admiralty saying rather casually that I should be hearing no more of the matter, as other arrangements had been made. Soon after it became known that Herstmonceux Castle had been bought, which was anyhow in the market.

The end of the war in Europe was now well in sight; on 7th May the German government agreed to unconditional surrender, and it was announced that 8th May was to be celebrated as V.E. Day. It happened to synchronize with my two days' leave from the Foreign Office, so I was able to organize a celebration at Hinton. Feverishly we built as large a bonfire as was possible at short notice on a high point of the ridge between the villages of Hinton and Bramdean, and from the local pub I was able to obtain a barrel of beer. As it grew dark a large concourse from the two villages assembled and at 10.30 precisely the barrel was broached and I set fire to the bonfire. It burned magnificently, the first flames of joy, as opposed to sorrow, that had lit the night sky for five and three-quarter years. From the ridge the dark landscape stretched away northward and southward into the invisible distance. The deep blue scene was suddenly broken by many little points of brilliant light where others all over the countryside were doing as we were, and celebrating the joyful end of the long succession of sombre days. It was a moving sight, as moving I think as the clamorous jubilations in the streets of London. About midnight as the fire died down and the barrel of beer gave out, we dispersed to our homes, I to Hinton where once again after so long an interval I slept in my own bedroom. The ten camp-beds had been removed and one of adult size found for me. That there was no carpet and only black-out over the windows was no hardship: I was at home again at last.

Next day I had to return to London, but a few weeks later I was able to leave my job at the Foreign Office, without grave regrets on either side, and devote myself to the exciting business of making Hinton more or less habitable again. The furniture was brought out of the harness-room, where the damp of nearly six years of storage had had a far from beneficial effect, while when the contents of the library emerged it became clear that large quantities of moth had spent an exceedingly well-fed war. However, the dilapidated chattels were put about so that a few of the rooms assumed a fairly domestic air.

The maculated condition of the walls naturally did not greatly help the general appearance, but after so long a tenancy by the school the condition of the house could not have been expected to be good. I had anticipated finding the walls covered with *graffiti* which might have formed an interesting study of child psychology; but I was disappointed. Perhaps they had been carefully erased. All I learnt, from a cellar door, was that Miss So-and-So was a So-and-So, and, in another childish hand in another quiet place, that a different Miss So-and-So was also a So-and-So. My studies were thus not highly productive.

The mood of rejoicing for peace soon passed, and those baffling years followed when the only improvement in the way of life seemed to be the release from danger from bombs. Ration cards and tickets continued when adjacent countries, France and Ireland, were suffering none of these restrictions. My particular problem was how to rehabilitate the house. I had been paid a small sum by the school for dilapidations, but I was not allowed to use it in doing any redecoration. It seemed a long time before I was able to paint or paper a single room, and at each application I usually received a permit for one room only. Gradually, however, the house began to look fairly respectable, but 1949 arrived and the drawing-room was still in the state it had been left by the school—stains on the walls, a large patch on the ceiling and cornice where a bath had overflowed, furrows on the Norfolk House boards of the floor where a grand piano had been pushed backwards and forwards, and so forth—and a permit for restoration was not forthcoming. At last I heard from a firm which was prepared to do the work without a permit. This was strictly against the law, but I trust that the Statute of Limitations holds and that I cannot now be prosecuted for accepting the offer.

The work had to be carried out in considerable secrecy: no prying eyes were to see what was being done. The drawing-room was accordingly cleared, and the men arrived with paint pots, ladders, trestles and all the necessary impedimenta. They worked long hours from eight in the morning till nine at night, and, since it was January and the days were short, a great part of their work was done by electric light. Unfortunately it had occurred to none of us that this large room with five uncurtained windows and a bay blazing with light for several hours each evening would be clearly visible for miles around. What has been happening at Hinton? I was asked by many neighbours who had observed our clandestine operation in progress, and I was forced to give some mumbling and prevaricating reply. Anyhow the room was completed, without police intervention, and looked with its yellow, striped paper extremely well.

During the following decade I was able by sundry purchases gradually to improve the standard of the contents. A certain amount of heavy furniture which had survived from the Victorian house was eliminated and replaced by more attractive things. The drawing-room, however, was allowed to retain a Victorian atmosphere. The rather clumsy white marble chimney-pieces, of which there were two, had been permitted to survive the alterations, with the 1867 cornices and mouldings, including a large plaster star in the Tudor manner in the centre of the ceilings in the south and north sections of the rooms. My grandparents' canary and Prussian blue curtains were adapted to the new shape of the windows, and the vast Edwin Long family group and some other far from interesting nineteenth-century copies of portraits were hung on the walls. A giltwood Hepplewhite suite of settee and chairs covered with the boldest and most brilliant Victorian grospoint, and a nineteenth-century Donegal carpet strewn with cabbage roses provided agreeable pattern and colour.

It must be owned that the room bore little resemblance to its appearance in my grandmother's day. Indeed it was as unlike a typical Victorian room as a Gothic Revival building, such as Strawberry Hill, was to its mediaeval prototype. However, it was light, gay and quite pretty, and I felt I had been right in retaining the nineteenth-century detail when almost all else in the house aimed at the eighteenth century or Regency periods. The library was very successfully designed by Lord Gerald Wellesley in the latter style, with pilasters, marbled like porphyry to marry with the chimney-piece, rising between recessed bookcases, from a marbled skirting.

The dining-room which, as has been said, was an entirely new room, created in the pre-war alterations, had worked out satisfactorily. The proportions were to some degree dictated by circumstances in that its width had to equal that of the drawing room while its depth was much less. The measurements were 27 feet by 21 feet, while its height was adjusted to the floor area; thus it was 2½ feet lower than the the drawing-room but about 18 inches higher than the other ground-floor rooms in the original Georgian block.

The painting of the Adam ceiling had to be delayed until the time when permits were no longer required, for it was not urgent work. At the time of the demolition of 37 Berkeley Square the ceiling had been painted white with the raised design gilded. This was not the original intention, and no doubt had been carried out in the nineteenth century. Fortunately Robert Adam's coloured drawing for the ceiling exists in the Soane Museum, and very brilliant in colouring it is, far more dominant in fact than we nowadays would find it comfortable to live with. However, it formed an admirable guide, and with the colours softened to our less robust taste, the ceiling when completed looked very attractive.

Thus 15 years passed since the war had ended, and the house had reached the state which I had had in mind when work on the transformation of the Victorian building had been begun in 1936. How lightheartedly I had set out, and with what excitement, mercifully having no knowledge of the difficulties and delays which were to beset the proper completion of the scheme. The operation which I had supposed would take about three years had in fact been drawn out to over 20—a very large slice of a life— but I now looked forward to being free from any major operations on the house for the remainder of my days. But disaster was at hand.

On Sunday, 3rd April 1960, the weather was particularly unpleasant. There was hardly a trace of spring in the countryside, and a strong south-east wind, almost a gale, was blowing beneath a grey, watery sky. After lunch my inclination was to sit by the fire and read the Sunday papers, but this I felt would be self-indulgent, so instead I went out to the woods for a little beneficial manual labour. Seldom was virtue worse rewarded. As I returned across the park an hour and a half later, I saw to my surprise a thin column of smoke rising above the trees from a position apparently in front of the house. Could this be a misplaced bonfire, I wondered? As I came nearer I suddenly saw through the shrubs of the garden sharp tongues of flame shining brilliantly beyond the bushes.

The catastrophe was now obvious: the house was on fire. I rushed across the garden and found firemen already at work tackling the flames which were for ever spreading. It seemed inconceivable that the house which I had left serene and tranquil so short a time before should now be engulfed in such terrible convulsions. Many more fire engines and firemen soon roared up, and a concourse gathered, for a fire is inevitably a public occasion. There arose the usual difficulty in country-house fires: a lack of water. The main water produced no more than a moderate supply, although it was turned off from neighbouring villages, much to their inconvenience. All the rainwater tanks and the formal pool were soon emptied, and eventually it was found necessary to carry a pipe down the drive and across the main road to a stream in meadows nearly half a mile away.

Meanwhile the flames fanned by the strong wind spread at a prodigious rate, their terrifying power seeming impossible to halt. At first the fire was contained within the library, where it had started, the books and the thick Georgian walls formed temporarily a barrier, but soon it burst through the ceiling and soared upwards to spread like a mushroom through the attics and so down again into the first-floor bedrooms below them. From outside one could watch room after room being consumed by the flames, and one thought with despair of the contents awaiting their inevitable destruction. Had one realized from the first that almost the whole house would be consumed, it would have been possible to save at least part of the drawing-room furniture, but soon the room was filled with black, putrid smoke, and it would have meant instant suffocation to go into it. The contents of my sitting-room, however, we managed to pass out through the windows although both ceiling and floor were smouldering, and thus not only many papers but also a few of my favourite possessions survived.

It was soon obvious that the whole of the main part of the house was doomed, and the firemen courageously stood in heat and smoke on the roof of the service wing attempting to prevent the flames spreading to that part. With the wind driving from the south-east it seemed a faint hope; but quite suddenly the wind, having successfully aided the destruction of all the main rooms, veered to the south-west and the wing was structurally saved, although it was naturally completely blackened with grime and water.

As it grew dark it was clear that the fire was under control. Here and there patches of flame were still destroying the woodwork but the horrifying force of the fire was spent and the air was gradually clearing of the thick nauseous clouds of smoke, which had poured from the ruined building for the past few hours. Before midnight there was nothing more to be done. A token force of firemen remained on the site in case of another outbreak, and I went to kind neighbours who housed me for the night.

The return to the house next morning was for me the worst moment of the disaster. During the fire the general tumult had been so great, the whole situation seemed so improbable that one's feelings were numbed by the noise and bustle, but to see in the morning light the gutted blackened structure with gaping windows through which appeared scenes of unbelievable chaos of fallen beams, partly destroyed furniture, mutilated books, was bitter indeed. While from the ruins emanated that despairing stench, that one had come to know all too well in wartime London, of burnt paint and sodden plaster.

On the terrace in front of the house stood the few dejected objects it had been possible to rescue during the fire. These were hurried away into an outbuilding where they were joined by a heterogeneous collection of furniture, objects, pictures which had somehow escaped complete destruction, and seemed perhaps capable of restoration. We found that a large part of the contents of the dining-room was not irreparably damaged as the fire had been stopped as it was descending through the ceiling, while some of the furniture in the ante-drawing-room was not a complete loss. Strangely enough a vast Dresden china clock beneath a glass dome, one of my grandmother's unwise purchases, had survived undamaged.

China, indeed, I was to find as we searched the ruins, had emerged from the ordeal far more successfully than anything made of marble. It was no doubt accustomed to heat, while marble had not experienced it for aeons. Porphyry, one of the hardest of marbles, seemed particularly susceptible, and I could find no trace at all amongst the cinders of the Library chimney-piece which had been my pride.

It was in this grate that the fire had started. There seemed no doubt that a spark from the logs had leapt over the guard and settled on a sofa which was near. Had it fallen on the carpet it would merely have burnt a hole, but materials and cushions are highly inflammable and by the time smoke was smelt the room was burning fiercely.

Hardly a book survived the conflagration. A few which were in my sitting-room emerged unburnt but so saturated with water as to be almost useless. Even when the print was still legible, the stained and twisted aspect of the covers was so repellent, and so unwelcome a reminder of the disaster, that I found it impossible to keep them. In the library every book was destroyed, and also those in a reference library housed in an attic. The former, subjected to intense heat and water, had become almost petrified as if engulfed by a volcanic eruption, and had to be hewn out of the bookcases with pickaxes.

It must be owned that a fire of this magnitude provides one benefit—an immense amount of useless material is destroyed. Whoever has the task of going through papers after my death should feel grateful that the work has been greatly lightened by the flames, and that the amount of lumber has been so effectively reduced.

From the moment that it became clear that the house was practically destroyed, I decided that I would rebuild with the minimum delay. The house was of little real architectural importance, and since the strong outer walls survived, it could be rebuilt so that there would be little alteration in its appearance. It had always been the site and the surroundings which provided the principal charms of the place and with these intact, I hoped that in a year or two the situation would be restored. About the eventual result I was correct: about the length of time required to achieve it I was foolishly optimistic.

Most fortunately Mr. Trenwith Wills who, with Lord Gerald Wellesley, had been the architect of the 1936 alterations was still in practice. I contacted him at once, and within 24 hours of the fire Mr. and Mrs. Wills were surveying the ruins and discussing plans with me for restoration. Within a very short time the scene in the forecourt returned almost exactly to that of 24 years earlier. The huts, the contractor's tackle, the ladders and scaffolding and a great quantity of essential paraphernalia.

Once again, as on the previous occasion, we concentrated first on rendering the domestic wing habitable, making the roof watertight, restoring the services, and of course repainting and papering from top to bottom to eradicate the hideous black stains and the stench of despair. A few weeks after the fire I was able to inhabit two small rooms on the ground floor which were to be my home for the next three years.

The domestic wing completed, work was turned to clearing the main body of the house of the vast quantity of débris and leaving only those parts which were still sound. In the dining-room section destruction was only partial, and over this a temporary roof was erected, but in the remainder there only survived within the outer shell a few lengths of internal wall on the ground floor: all else had to be carted away as rubbish. Amongst the latter were many broken pieces of the collection of porphyry ornaments, but now indistinguishable in the dust and grime from pieces of broken brick, so all—precious marble and humble brick —went to form a useful foundation for a new cattle-yard at the Home Farm. Perhaps one day the porphyry will come to light again and it will be deduced that there must on this spot have been an important Roman settlement.

This first phase occupied six months, and it was not until

October that the shell of the house had been completely cleared of all damaged brickwork and timber, and the site was ready for rebuilding—the fifth rebuilding that had taken place at Hinton since the Tudor house had been erected sometime in the first half of the sixteenth century.

Thus I and the architects had had ample time to consider plans, but in fact we had decided on only one major alteration: this was that the attic floor, which had existed over the main part of the house, should not be replaced. The rather high Mansard roof with dormer windows showing over the parapet had always appeared a little too dominant, and furthermore the rooms contained in it had been barely used since the departure of the school. In re-instatement there was to be only one low attic covering the area of the original Georgian section of the house. Thus we were able to lower the height of the house by about 5 feet, and the chimneys as well which had anyhow to be rebuilt, and reduce the number of rooms by ten. In the reconstruction of 1936 we had eliminated the same number, so that the house was now brought to a quite moderate size.

In the interior the alterations were minor. Since almost all the Victorian features of the drawing-room had been destroyed, it seemed absurd to reconstruct it as a nineteenth-century room, for it must be owned that all the detail, chimney-pieces, cornices, door cases and so forth had been singularly clumsy and coarse, and had not married very happily with the Adelphi window linings which I had inserted in the previous rebuilding. The majority of these carved linings had survived, and it was they that formed the note for the new aspect. I was fortunate in finding two late eighteenth-century chimney-pieces, similar but not an exact pair, in which well-carved female figures support the shelf, and also a pair of rather fine door cases from the demolished house of Ashburnham; the rest of the detail, cornices, pillars and entablature between the two parts of the room are modern fibrous plaster of eighteenth century design.

No doubt there is much to be said against a restoration of this sort, indeed against the whole conception of rebuilding what was anyhow largely an eighteenth-century replica. Had I been young perhaps a house in contemporary idiom would have shown more enterprise, but I was not young, and a Georgian fabric was essential as a setting for the furniture and objects which I had every intention of collecting to replace all I had lost. Unquestionably, too, rather spacious eighteenth-century style rooms are both pleasant and practical to live in. So, without a qualm of conscience, I encouraged this atavistic work to proceed.

The library was restored almost exactly as before, but it was not easy to find a chimney-piece of suitable design, and I had given up hope of discovering one of porphyry as had been the previous one, when by good fortune, I found a suitable replacement in an *antiquaire* on the Quai Voltaire in Paris. It was of simple Louis XVI design in white marble inset with panels of porphyry. At the top of each jamb was the letter 'N' in white marble and in the middle of the frieze a beribboned crown. I was told that it had come from the demolished palace of Saint-Cloud, but even if this were true it seemed difficult to reconcile the pre-Revolution design with the Napoleonic initials. On consulting the history of the palace, however, I discovered that Marie-Antoinette had made alterations there shortly before 1790 which could account for the design, while Napoleon could have added his initial and crown—a reproduction in miniature of the crown which he set on his own head in the famous scene in Notre Dame—in order to impress his personality, as was his custom, on those palaces of the deposed Bourbons which he inhabited. Whether this illustrious *provenance* is genuine or not, the chimney-piece suits the humble setting of the library extremely well.

The dining-room, with half the Adam ceiling destroyed, presented in some ways an even more depressing spectacle than the two former rooms which had been reduced to bare walls, but we found that enough of the plasterwork had survived to reproduce the missing section. The gods and goddesses in the little pictures had disappeared for ever before the heat and water, and all had to be replaced. I was lucky to find a young artist, Elizabeth Biddulph, who caught the exact sentiment of these small Olympian scenes and the new paintings have the proper eighteenth-century flavour. Thus the room returned to its original appearance and contains a good deal of its former furniture, but all required drastic restoration.

In the entrance hall from which these rooms open only one feature survived, and this was the massive porphyry chimney-piece. It was completely blackened and rather damaged, and appeared at first sight to be beyond repair, but Messrs Fenning, the marble masons, were of the opinion that it could be restored, so it was taken out and sent to their works at Putney Bridge whence, after many months, it emerged in apparently pristine condition. Messrs Fenning also carry on the art of making scagliola, the composition which so closely resembles marble as to be almost indistinguishable from it. Before very long four handsome Ionic columns in semblance of *serpentino verde* with porphyry bases, and with attendant pilasters, had arrived on the site for setting up in the hall. These were erected on a floor of black and white marble, large white squares with small black set diagonally, also provided by Messrs Fenning from plans worked out with minute accuracy by Trenwith Wills. The laying of the floor was not a simple operation, and was one which gave considerable trouble, but it was highly rewarding when finished since, besides looking handsome, it greatly lightened the room which had previously been rather dark.

Not a vestige of the original staircase survived, and one assumes it must have made admirable food for the flames. It was in any case of no beauty as it had been adapted from the Victorian stair. The new one follows the same lines, but has more grace, and also mounts only to the first floor instead of into the now vanished attics. It leads on the first floor to a landing which is given architectural interest by the spanning of each side with wide three-centred arches, while at the end of the short passage leading to the bedrooms over the drawing-room a tall niche was made to form a terminal feature. This was marbled verde-antique and in it was set a white marble vase: it is quite an effective little arrangement. In the opposite direction a passage leads away past a middle stair on the north side and the door to the bedroom over the dining-room, and so to the service wing.

None of the planning on this floor was materially altered as it had always been satisfactory, and there was a generous supply of bathrooms, but by minor changes it was so arranged that every bedroom had a bathroom opening out of it. Since all the floors had disappeared in the fire we were able to make one improvement which had not been feasible in the 1936 rebuilding. By lowering the ceiling of the drawing-room a few inches and lessening its thickness slightly, it was possible to bring the floors of the bedrooms in this section into happier relation with the windows. Before the fire the bottom sill had been only 6 inches or so from the floor, now it was 14 inches; while in the central section, by a reverse manoeuvre, the sills were just under 2½ feet from the floor instead of 6 inches higher. There is no doubt that the height of windows in a room is a matter of importance. In the Victorian house they had been so extremely ill-placed that I was sensitive on the point.

While on this subject, it is perhaps worth mentioning that all floors are non-inflammable, they are indeed what is known professionally as 'pot floors'. They are constructed in the following way: steel girders (R.S.J.s to the initiated) cross from wall to wall and between them are set re-inforced concrete joists about 1 foot apart; between the joists come the 'pots', that is to say large hollow bricks. Naturally each floor has to be individually measured, so that R.S.J.s, joists and pots fit like pieces of a puzzle. On the top of this is a layer of cement to keep all in place, and above the cement the floor boards—impregnated against fire like all the new timber—are laid on thin battens. There is thus none of the unpleasant rigidity which is inevitable in a solid concrete floor. All this is perhaps not of general interest, but it is a system devised so that fire, should it break out, would be contained within the room where it started. I sincerely trust I may never have to test the efficacy of the construction.

As the structure neared completion it was necessary to consider the decoration and furnishing of all the rooms. Ever since the fire I had been buying furniture, objects and pictures to replace all that had disappeared, and since the form of the rooms was as before it was not an impossible task to acquire what was suitable. I had also bought carpets, for I was anxious that every room should have a carpet of character. But the choice of colour schemes, materials for curtains and so forth was almost beyond my ability, and my unguided taste would probably have led to disaster. However, a guide was at hand in my friend Ronald Fleming, and with his invaluable help the decoration of each room was built up from the colouring in the carpets which I had obtained. The result of our co-operation was highly successful, and the house has, I think, regained the mellow atmosphere it had before the fire, and it is difficult to believe that only a short time ago it was a blackened ruin. Exactly three years and one month after the fire, in May 1963, the house was once again fully habitable.

The Garden   I

In writing about the garden at Hinton and in giving some account of its development over the past 30 years or so, I must at the outset confess, before it becomes too obvious to the expert, that I am not a very knowledgeable plantsman. But starting as I did in the early '30s with almost no experience at all, I have come to know, often by unexpected reverses, which plants will and which will not consent to grow in the poor limey soil at Hinton, and also how to treat them so that they give as good a display as I can hope for. I have still much to learn, but I intend to continue adding to my knowledge as long as I am *compos mentis*.

My interest lies, I think, more in shrubs than in flowers, and perhaps more in trees than in either of the two former, but it seems to me that it is essential to use all three in harmony in order to form an attractive and successful garden. I have learnt during the past years what above all I want from a garden: this is tranquillity. It is a quality which most gardens can have whether they are of the 'cottagey' sort with an ordered confusion of plants or designed on broad formal lines as at Hinton. It is achieved by the avoidance of harsh and brilliant colours such as strident oranges and scarlets, or by violent contrasts. It seems strange that so many new roses are produced of these difficult shades, but presumably they are generally popular; and a garden such as that at Hinton, where the colouring is in a low key, may seem to many to be decidedly lacking in display.

I have said that the soil is limey. That is perhaps describing it too kindly for in places, particularly on the east side of the garden, solid chalk comes to within a few inches of the surface. Elsewhere there is a depth of a foot or more of loam above the chalk, while here and there are pockets of the coldest clay—wet and sodden in winter, dry and cracked in summer. Away on the north side of the garden is an area of good deep loam, where the chalk has vanished far down. This small piece of ground I shall describe later, but it is provoking to see how luxuriantly plants grow here compared with their behaviour in the major part of the garden.

The soil, then, is a drawback, but the site, as I have said in the first chapter, is a definite asset. The ground slopes gently southward with a wide landscape spread out before it. The wind is a trial, for shelter from the south-west gales, which are the strongest if not the coldest, cannot be obtained without obscuring the view; in compensation, however, the beds below the terrace walls receive any sunshine that there may be.

I think, too, that the garden at Hinton has another advantage, and since it is, like the site, in no way a work of mine, I feel I may be allowed to praise it. It is this: it has a great sense of antiquity. This comes from the fact that there has been a house and garden on the site for centuries; and of course the venerable trees, of which there are a good many, are conducive to this atmosphere. But it is not this alone, for houses are often built on sites where good trees are standing and yet a feeling of maturity is not there. The sense of antiquity is indefinable, and perhaps to many imperceptible, but it exists, and I think that Hinton in spite of the fact that the garden has been so altered and expanded in the past 30 years, and that the house has been twice rebuilt in this time, has this sense in large measure.

It is impossible to say when a garden was first made on the site, but vestigial remains of the layout surrounding the Tudor house still survive. The main kitchen garden, with walls surrounding just an acre of ground, was certainly created before the old building was demolished in 1793, as it is on the same axis and must almost have adjoined its western side. The north wall of the garden was exactly in line with the north front of the house, and below these two ran a long terrace, the form of which is still apparent, although it is now partly obscured by shrubs. This terrace was no doubt the bowling green which was detailed in the Parliamentary survey of 1649, as mentioned in the first chapter. The drive which was made by my parents in the first years of this century down to the main road in the valley to the north cuts through it.

The terrace may have formed an excellent bowling green, but must have been a chilly spot facing north and shaded from the sun by the house and the walls of the kitchen-garden. However, our ancestors seem to have been more pre-occupied with keeping cool than warm, as the aspect of their houses often shows, so this shady green may have suited them. From this terrace there was an agreeable view northwards over a stretch of park-land descending rather steeply into the valley along which now runs the Winchester to Petersfield highway. Beyond the valley the ground rises to the long Lamborough ridge, and to the wide area on which the Battle of Cheriton was fought, as has already been described in a previous chapter.

This part of the park lying to the north and north-west of the house was always called by my father the Deer Park, but when it obtained this ambitious name I do not know, for it is neither as extensive nor as bosky as this name would suggest. It does, however, contain a few trees of great age, of which three squat and massive oaks appear to be the most venerable. It is impossible to make an even faintly accurate guess at the age of these trees, and the hopeful suggestion that oaks or yews may be a thousand years old is generally wide of the mark. In the case of the Hinton oaks I would hazard an age of anything between 500 and 700 years. The trunks are now more or less hollow, and the girth of the largest at 5 feet from the ground is 21 feet 10 inches. This is no record—there are a number in the country larger—but it is a respectable size. A photograph of this tree taken about 1860 shows that the change in its outline in the course of a century is negligible.

The Tudor house was inhabited by the Stewkeley family and the Stawells for two centuries until the demolition in 1793, and since they were far from poor one would expect that there would have been some attempt to lay out a garden in the formal Dutch style which came into fashion after the Restoration of 1660. The Survey made of the Manor House in 1649, which has been quoted in an earlier chapter, mentions sundry courtyards and these may have been developed into a formal layout of some sort. But there now remains only one feature, and this is a narrow avenue of lime trees which extended opposite the front door of the house southward down the slope to the edge of the steep bank which formed the boundary of the park and also of the parish.

In a map of the county made in 1759 the avenue is shown, so one must suppose that the trees by that date were large enough to record, thus they were probably planted about 1720. The avenue was 'clumped' into three groups probably when the Georgian house was built in 1793, a period when formal avenues were out of fashion and when in any case the avenue leading to a no-longer existing front door must have seemed purposeless. Now the slowly decaying veterans of the clumps still stand, showing that limes are not short-lived, and as will be described later they have been worked into the scheme of the garden.

These sparse details are all that survive of the surroundings of the vanished house, and as with the building itself they were allowed to disappear into oblivion without so much, apparently, as an amateur's watercolour to record their existence. When the new house was built on a site 60 yards to the south, just below the crest of the hill, formal gardens were entirely outdated and the principles of Capability Brown prescribed that the rough turf of parks should sweep up to the very walls of country houses. With enthusiasm landowners followed the new trend and swept away the walls and clipped hedges of the Stuart layouts round their houses and the avenues across their parks, and in their place endeavoured to create a scene that appeared both natural and romantic.

At Hinton, which was no more than a modest manor house, there seems to have been little to destroy, and equally the last Lord Stawell made small attempt by planting to give any romance to the park and, indeed, as the area was not great it would anyhow have been difficult. Furthermore, since the new house was turned slightly to the westward while the Tudor house faced exactly north and south, any existing formality would have found itself entirely adrift, and only the kitchen garden and the stables, which were concealed by a shrubbery were able unobtrusively to survive.

The 1793 house can have depended on little except trees for its setting and on its view as an additional amenity. From the steep lane which led up the hill from the highway, a drive entered the precincts by the church and swept in a wide curve through a shrubbery to reach the front door directly from the east; while those making for the back door followed the line of the present drive, which skirts the churchyard wall and passes the site of the demolished house and the stables, and so reaches the kitchen yard, being kept discreetly out of sight behind bushes.

Along the south side of the house ran a narrow terrace, raised above the level of the park by a wall. Perhaps the pleasure of sunshine was already beginning to be appreciated, for undoubtedly this terrace, and in fact the general aspect of the house, must have been more agreeable than anything in the building it replaced. On the north-east side of the house a grove of beech trees was planted which is now highly effective in providing protection from the coldest winds and maybe that for this and for a number of lime trees less than two centuries old I should be grateful to Lord Stawell.

I do not think that either of my grandparents were particularly interested in gardens, and indeed the enthusiasm for horticulture which is so widespread nowadays is a comparatively modern development. But as long ago as 1841 Mrs. Loudon published her highly successful book *Gardening for Ladies*, which stimulated an interest in many women who had previously supposed that work in a garden could only be done by those who were paid to do it, and that the nearest the lady of the house could come to manual labour was to cut a few roses for the drawing-room. Mrs. Loudon's book, with its admirable advice, suggested that there was nothing demeaning about working in a garden, and that the most elegant women with the aid of gloves, secateurs and trowels could make themselves very useful amongst their shrubs and flowers. This notion would have startled Jane Austen whose heroines confined their useful activities to indoor work and restricted their outside exercise to walking.

Thus although both knowledge and interest in gardening was developing during the middle decades of the nineteenth century, it does not appear to have been a subject which impinged very seriously on my grandparents. But having rebuilt their house in 1867 on an ambitious scale, it was obvious that the restricted surroundings of the Georgian house were entirely inadequate as a setting for the Victorian Tudor mansion, and that more extensive 'pleasure grounds' were essential. In order to achieve this they decided on a number of quite bold undertakings.

On the north side the drive, which had approached the front door of the Georgian house, was reduced in width and importance to no more than a gravel garden path winding between laurels and aucubas, while in front of the house a large, roughly rectangular forecourt was dug out of the rising ground and was reached from the service drive through a narrow opening. A sea of laurels was planted on either side of this opening so that any tradesman's trap on its way to the back door would be only momentarily visible from the front. The wide expanse of gravel was carried up to the very walls of the house, so that there was no fringe of grass or shrubs to soften the austerity of the architecture.

Besides its ugliness there was a practical objection to this bleak parade ground which my grandparents had not envisaged: it formed an all-too efficient catchment area. Only inadequate drains had been provided, so that after a heavy storm, water poured down the slope to the house and flooded through gratings into the cellars. Larger drains still failed to solve the problem, and I remember when I was young that it was not a rare sight after a heavy thunderstorm to find a sombre sea upwards of a foot deep covering the cellar floors. When I altered the house in 1936 I reduced the area of the forecourt and gave it symmetry by laying a wide stretch of turf against the house and this, although carried out for appearance, was effective in keeping back the storm water.

The construction of the forecourt entailed digging out many tons of soil, here heavy clay, and this was deposited to the south-east of the house so as to form a level roughly rectangular platform about 30 yards by 20. Round it were planted the inevitable laurels interspersed with yew trees and ilex, while to the south a flight of narrow steps was built down the long slope to a grass path below. A garden of sorts was thus beginning to take shape.

This platform with its sheltering evergreens seemed the obvious place for the planting of a rose garden, and a little layout was made for this purpose. Two gravel paths were made crossing from side to side with a circular bed at their intersection, and standard rose trees in little pools of open earth alternated with variegated maples. In the four quarters thus formed were a number of odd-shaped beds planted with hybrid tea roses, while on the east side stood a pair of weeping ash, their pendant branches trained over iron frames like the whalebone beneath the crinolines which were currently in fashion. As they grew they formed in summer agreeable arbours into which dappled green sunlight percolated through the foliage.

This garden remained unaltered when I was a small boy, and was quite an attractive example of mid-Victorian design, of which Mrs. Loudon would on the whole have approved. There was, however, one unfortunate drawback: the roses were always a failure. The fallacy that hybrid teas will thrive in any sort of clay dies hard, and both my grandmother and my mother remained convinced that this little garden contained exactly the soil that roses needed. But in fact the heavy impermeable and lime-impregnated ground filled the unfortunate little plants with almost instant despair, and a wet winter condemned them to nearly certain death by drowning. But these reverses were optimistically attributed to the choice of the wrong varieties, and every two years or so another batch of little victims was procured which inevitably died away in a season or two. However, this was the rose garden and roses it must contain, although the beds of moribund twigs could hardly be said to give much visual pleasure.

My grandparents' other extension to the garden was on the south side of the house where they replaced the retaining wall of the terrace by a grass bank and formed two long grass terraces with another low bank between them. From the lower of these a ramshackle flight of wooden and grass steps led down another steep bank to an area of mown lawn ornamented with two Thuyas and sundry small beds filled in summer with the inevitable scarlet geraniums and lobelia. This area was separated from the park by a high iron fence, along which ran a mown path leading on the east to the steps descending from the rose garden, and on the west petering out beneath the branches of a group of horse chestnuts.

It is thus that I remember the garden in my earliest years, when it still remained almost exactly as my grandparents had made it, except for an added maturity, 25 or 30 years before. My father had no interest at all in the garden, indeed he resented the expense of maintaining something which seemed to him unnecessary. The growing of some vegetables and the mowing of an area of lawn close to the house would have been to him fully adequate. My mother, although no plantswoman, had a strong sense of the setting required for a rather large house, but with the difficulties of running the house and bringing up a family the garden during the first decades of her marriage had little of her attention.

She made alterations, however, in the rose garden. This, from having been typically mid-Victorian in design, and so, to the taste of today, rather charming, became at the turn of the century obviously old fashioned. To my mother it seemed fussy and crowded, which undoubtedly it was, and something simpler and bolder was more to the taste of the dawning Edwardian era. Thus the weeping ashes, the maples, the standard roses were all swept away, and the many little beds were replaced by four large ones, one in each quarter, while round the central bed a circle of posts supported alternately Dorothy Perkins and Crimson Rambler roses. The new beds were, of course, again planted with hybrid teas, which in due course wilted and died as before. The new arrangement had at least one unquestionable merit, it was easier of upkeep.

In 1912, when my parents' financial position must have been easier than it had been during the earlier years of their marriage, although my father would never for one instant have admitted that this was the case, my mother undertook a bold and quite expensive alteration in the garden. Probably the greater part of the cost came from her own resources, as I hardly suppose my father would have made more than a token contribution.

This undertaking consisted of uniting the two long narrow terraces below the south front of the house into a single broad sward, and containing the far side with a brick wall topped by a stone balustrade. Much thought was given to finding a suitable design for the latter, and since the house was Tudoresque in style—in so far as it was anything—my mother concluded that something with a Tudor flavour would be appropriate. She consulted the illustrated books on gardens and country houses published by Country Life, such as *Gardens Old and New*, and *In English Homes*, and in one of these found a design that pleased her. This was accordingly reproduced. The original was no doubt attractive, but the reproduction was coarse and heavy in execution, and I regret she did not decide on simple eighteenth-century style balusters.

Basically, however, the scheme was a good one. The single wide terrade was a decided improvement, while from the windows of the house the balustrade, in spite of its clumsiness, agreeably framed the view and gave it an added depth and recession. But unfortunately there were drawbacks which mitigated against the success of the alteration. For one thing my father's croquet lawn, which was at the east end of the house, jutted out on a higher level into the new terrace, and could not possibly be curtailed, and so formed an aggressive promontory; and for another there was the difficulty of finding a suitable axis for building the balustrade in front of an entirely unsymmetrical house. In the end it was vaguely centralized on the unequal bow-windows of the drawing room and dining-room with the result that the central steps, which in any case were too steep, and too narrow, had no relation with the house at all, and in fact this was the trouble with the whole balustrade.

There was another difficulty which I had not appreciated until I came to alter the house in 1936. The builders of the balustrade had taken their measurements from the fronts of the two bow-windows, not realizing that that of the drawing-room projected about 18 inches further forward than the other. The balustrade, therefore, was never parallel to the main body of the house, and this when I began to develop the garden in later years worried me considerably. However, so inexact is the human eye that I believe this inaccuracy in the layout is not generally apparent.

My parents were not fortunate in their choice of head gardeners and a succession of incompetent men were in charge. Perhaps their incompetence was due to the lack of knowledge of their employers, and certainly from my father they received no stimulus whatever. But in 1931 my mother (my father was then 84 and took no part in the proceedings) by some miracle secured the services of a young man, Walter Holloway, who was a gardener of remarkable gifts. Had he lived he would have gone far in his profession, but in 1937—two years after my father's death—he died after an operation for acute appendicitis. I grieved for him deeply, both as a friend and as an employee, and I shall always be grateful to him for having stimulated in me an enthusiasm for gardens which I had barely had before I knew him. In the few years he had worked at Hinton he had lifted the garden out of the dreary rut it had been in for so long as I could remember, and was beginning to give it interest and beauty.

In the following year I had the great good fortune to find Herbert Gray to take his place, who now, almost 30 years later, is still with me. Together, in perfect harmony and with the aid of a band of admirable assistants, we labour constantly to improve the standard of the garden. We are both fully aware that the condition of a garden can never remain stationary: if it does not go forward, it goes back. In fact we know in the words of the Red Queen that 'it takes all the running you can do to keep in the same place', so we continue to run as fast as our increasing age will allow.

In January 1935 my father died within three weeks of his

88th birthday, but some years before his death he had prudently handed over to me capital which provided sufficient income to pay the gardeners' wages, so that the control of the garden had for some time been in my hands. A year before his death he had agreed to my making what was the first material alteration I had undertaken. I had happily made a couple of hundred pounds on the Stock Exchange, so I was able to carry out the work without financial assistance, but it was an achievement to obtain his consent, particularly as my plan entailed the removal of the escarpment caused by the croquet lawn, which in any case had not been used for several years.

I had already taken to heart the well-known lines of Alexander Pope in his *Epistle to the Earl of Burlington*:

> *Let not each beauty ev'ry where be spy'd,*
> *Where half the skill is decently to hide;*
> *He gains all points, who pleasingly confounds,*
> *Surprizes, varies, and conceals the Bounds.*

These sagacious words where directed to the laying out of parks on the grand scale, but can be applied with equal force to gardens. The garden at Hinton at that time, it must be owned, did not fulfil a single one of these directions and my enterprise in 1934 was an attempt to carry into effect at least the last three words of the quatrain.

To this end the earth from the croquet lawn was wheeled to a position below my mother's balustrade so as to form on this slightly sloping site the raised south side of a sunken garden; a brick wall 18 inches high was built round the garden, and a yew hedge was planted round three sides, with the balustrade closing the fourth. I am not inclined to think that this, my first attempt at landscape gardening, was an overwhelming success, but it achieved two of the objectives I had in mind. Firstly the little terrace on the south side topped by the yew hedge effectively 'concealed the Bounds', in that the severe iron fence which formed the boundary between park and garden was no longer in full view, and would be completely hidden as soon as the hedge grew; and secondly there was now an effective wind-break so that the four oblong beds within the sunken garden were well protected. Until this alteration was made the beds were exposed to the full force of the south-west wind and flowers such as tulips were often decapitated in quantities just as they were reaching perfection.

If the sunken garden was not a very striking achievement, a further alteration which stemmed from it was, if I may praise my own work, quite satisfactory. This was the formation of a grass path, long and wide, from the eastern edge of the garden to the western, a total length of over 200 yards, which passed midway through the sunken garden. It was not an altogether easy operation: there were several large trees to be considered and also a tennis court, cut into the slope some years earlier, which butted into the line which seemed indicated. However, these obstacles were overcome: the trees were negotiated, the tennis court was shortened by a few feet without detriment, and we then found that the path at its east end would centre very happily on a large Irish yew.

Even so the work was considerable, for a formal path, such as this was intended to be, must be perfectly level from side to side. That it should rise or fall in its length is no drawback, rather the reverse, but here the ground sloped slightly to the south so that a certain amount of digging out on one side and making up on the other was entailed. Along the western section of the path we planted an avenue of Irish yews, fifteen on either side, and I foresaw that in years to come the effect would be quite noble. At the time, however, these lines of 3 feet trees looked rather absurd, while the fact that the path ended in an ordinary farm gate into the park increased the bathos. It was not until more than a decade later, after the war, that I was able to replace the gate with a cattle-grid so that the eye was carried unimpeded along the path and out into the park, thus once again 'concealing the Bounds'. About the same time as we made the cattle-grid I found an eighteenth-century statue of Diana, which I set against the Irish yew at the east end, whence she gazes out over the garden to the wide landscape stretched before her.

From these first fumbling efforts at laying out a garden I learnt a great deal. I learnt that in a garden such as Hinton it was essential that the basic bone-structure should be conceived on logical grounds. When I took over there was no bone-structure at all, and no logic. Little extensions, little pools of interest, had been made here and there, but nothing led to anything else. There was in fact no overall plan. My constant intention, which I would hesitate to say has been fully successful, has been to make the garden 'flow', so that a visitor is led on from point to point, and vistas, long or short, come here and there into view.

A good basic plan seems particularly essential in a garden such as Hinton which is fairly large but where the soil is poor so that a very luxuriant effect is difficult to achieve. Satisfactory lines are some compensation for not very robust plants. I have had another principle in mind when developing the garden, which follows from the basic bone-structure, and this is to treat the garden as an artist, an old master let us say, would his canvas—to allow no dull or wasted areas. By this I do not mean that every part of the garden should be broken up with some planting or object to give interest, for in fact nothing is so satisfactory or peaceful as an area of plain lawn, but that every part should have some purpose, should be designed to have some visual effect. At Hinton I am inclined to believe that the most attractive area is the sward of plain lawn lying between the church and the house with the tall, jade-green stems of beech trees rising beyond it. There is spaciousness and tranquillity here, which my more elaborate efforts elsewhere have not achieved.

Tall deciduous trees are of course an immense help in giving a garden an agreeable atmosphere, and at Hinton there are fortunately a good many. But they have very obvious drawbacks. If they were planted when the layout of the garden was made, and one thinks of William Kent's masterly early eighteenth-century designs, they form a superb unity; but if the layout has to be adjusted to existing trees, it is a different matter. At Hinton many difficulties arose, and I have often thought how easy it must be to lay out a garden on a virgin site; but perhaps difficulties overcome in the end add interest, although to sacrifice a tree for the sake of a new path or shrub bed is always a painful decision.

In an earlier chapter I have described the rebuilding of the house between the years 1936 and 1938. These drastic alterations gave the main part of the house complete symmetry. The middle section, five bays wide, now reassumed the appearance it had presented when it was built, while it was flanked on either side by a pair of comfortable, semicircular bay-windows. In the centre was a French window, with an imposing architectural surround, and curving steps leading down to the top terrace. At last it was possible to base the garden properly on the house: when it was a jumble of mid-Victorian asymmetry the one could have no relation to the other.

The first feature to tackle was the balustrade, the embarrassing balustrade, which was now more adrift than ever, while in the new atmosphere of classical reason the design was completely out of place. I was in some doubt whether to remove it or so to alter it that it had a proper relation to the house. Another alternative would have been to take away the Tudor frets and replace them by balusters, but this was an undertaking I could not afford, and in any case I had become so accustomed to the design that, I think, its impact on me had lost its force.

In the end I decided to adjust it to the new form of the house, and this worked out fairly well. The central steps were moved a few feet westward and doubled in width and given an easier descent, and the balustrade was extended by several bays to conform with the new outline of the house. This entailed also enlarging the sunken garden lying below it to coincide with the lengthened balustrade. Now, with the clumsy stonework discreetly covered with climbing roses and clematis the general effect is not unattractive. More than a decade later the whole composition was improved by making a wide opening through the south side of the sunken garden and building steps down to a large semi-circular bastion retained by a wall extending out into the park. Thus an adequate foreground to the house was created, a feature it had previously singularly lacked.

With the outbreak of war and the taking over of the house by the Portsmouth Day School, it might have been supposed that all improvements would be at an end. But during that first sinister year of delayed hostilities the calling up of young men moved slowly, and the State showed no wish for the services of the younger gardeners. There was thus little to occupy them; and the headmistress of the school begged that they should be kept away from close proximity to the house as their presence, it seemed, distracted her little charges from their studies. I therefore decided to carry out an improvement which I had had in mind for some time, and which fortunately was on a site well out of view of the windows.

The plan was to make the remains of the old lime avenue, which had led up to the Tudor house, and now extended in a desultory way across the park, into a feature as seen from the

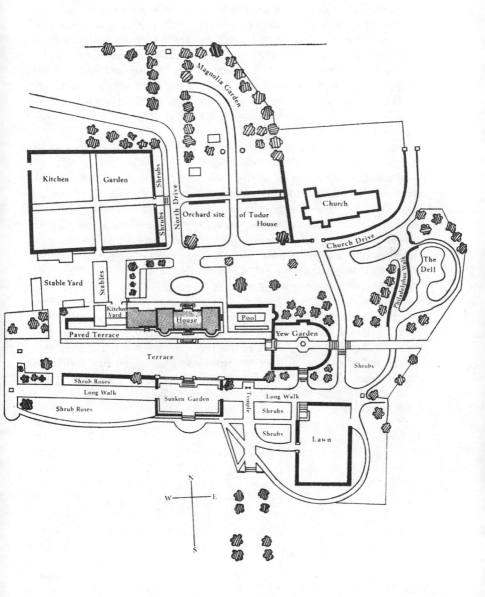

garden. To achieve this we made a broad grass path branching southward from the long east–west walk and aligned on the avenue. On either side of the path we made beds of shrubs, which now that the plants have grown, successfully guide the eye down the avenue. Various other paths were formed between the shrub beds, one taking a wide curve on to the former tennis court and another looping down below the steep bank of the court and rising again on the far side at the point where the statue of Diana was later to stand.

All this was successfully carried out and, though not very helpful to the war-effort, was successful, I believe, in fulfilling the headmistress's injunctions, but since I could rarely be at Hinton I knew little of what was occurring. Very soon all thoughts of improvements were at an end, and with the intensification of hostilities the upkeep of the garden was reduced to a minimum, the lawns became hayfields, the shrub beds and herbaceous borders a tangle of weeds, and nettles, ground elder and convolvulus flourished everywhere. Before one's eyes one could see how quickly a neglected garden reverts to a wilderness, and centuries of care and work can be wiped out in a year or two. Only the kitchen garden was kept properly in order, for here were grown the vegetables for the school. The yew hedges were my own special care, and each year when I had a week of summer leave from the Foreign Office I would come up to Hinton from my mother's house where I stayed and clip away for hours at a time. The work was not very expertly done, but at least the hedges were kept more or less in shape.

The Garden   II
Restoration and Development

Cℳℳℳ

The long sad years of the war eventually ended, the school returned to Portsmouth, and I was once again living at Hinton.
The first task in the garden was to reconvert the hayfield which
lay below the windows into a lawn. Motor scythes did not at that
time, I think, exist; at any rate we had none, nor indeed any
petrol had we possessed a machine. Thus there was no alternative
to cutting this rather large area by hand. Fortunately there were
two men, an elderly gardener and a woodman, who were prepared to undertake this exhausting work. During the long summer
evenings of July 1945 they would spend many hours in bringing
back order to the rough and flowery meadow which the lawn had
become.

They were expert scythers, and it was an extraordinary pleasure
to watch the swaths of tall weeds falling before the rhythmical
motions of the long blades. It was an occupation and an instru-
ment which had not altered over the centuries. Now, with so
many mechanical aids, the scythe is fast becoming an obsolete
tool. Perhaps before long, Father Time will be portrayed with a
mechanical apparatus to mow down his human harvest.

Thus the broad terrace was cleared of hay, but naturally several
years passed before it became once again one of those lawns which
are said to be the glory of English gardens. This work and the
general tidying up of the more visible parts of the garden was all
that it was possible to attempt during the first 12 months after
V.E. Day. And indeed there was a great deal to do, for not only
were there the weeds which nature had provided with generosity
during the past few years, but there were also the ravages which a

couple of hundred little feet careering about the garden had created.

Demobilization, however, was beginning, and first one, and then another man returned to the more congenial profession of gardening, and we were able to aim at restoring the place to a civilized appearance. The area which had perhaps suffered the most severely by unavoidable neglect was the Dell. It had always been so called, but it was in fact a small chalk-pit lying on the east side of the garden. It is impossible to say at what period it was excavated, and there are pits of this sort all about this area, but a large elm tree standing just within the entrance indicates that chalk must first have been dug here upwards of two centuries ago.

Originally the Dell lay outside the boundary of the garden, and a public footpath uniting the church of Hinton with that of Kilmeston a mile to the south, separated it from the garden. For many years it seems to have been used as a general rubbish dump, and all sorts of debris—broken china, bottle ends, and so forth—still makes its unwelcome appearance on the surface of the soil. My parents prudently arranged for the line of the footpath to be moved to the outside of the Dell, so that it was no longer a convenient place for disposal of rubbish from adjacent cottages. Instead it was used by the gardeners for the burning of weeds.

It had long seemed to me that the Dell had possibilities—capabilities Mr. Brown would have called them—and before the war we had begun to clear it of the saplings and nettles which choked it. A grass walk was carried into it leading to a small area of lawn covering the floor, and various shrubs were planted on the uncharitable slopes, uncharitable for in places they were sheer chalk. On the line of the former footpath we made a grass walk bordered by hedges of box which serpentines rather pleasantly following the lie of the land. Behind the hedges we planted *Philadelphus Grandiflora*, which although faint in scent grows tall, and now when in flower makes an impressive picture in the tranquil colouring of white and green. Behind the *Philadelphus* and so at the top of the slopes we planted sundry evergreens, yews, ilex, and so forth, with the intention that one day they would increase the apparent height of the slopes and so give a slight sense of drama to a site which in fact had very little.

Within a year of the beginning of the war, the Dell had to be abandoned to Nature, that most insensitive of gardeners when her activities are not severely controlled, and all the young shrubs and trees disappeared into a wilderness of nettles. The Dell, therefore, seemed a suitable place to begin rescue work as soon as labour was available. We soon found that all but the toughest plants had died from suffocation and lack of light, so, except for some of the evergreens at the top of the slopes, it was necessary to start the work of reclamation all over again.

' We redesigned to some degree the floor of the Dell, making beds for shrubs and plants with casual, curving shapes on either side of the central area of lawn, planning it, on its small scale, rather in the way that Capability Brown would have designed a lake, so that from the entrance one does not immediately perceive the end. It is a modest little deception. On the chalky slopes we deposited good top-soil dug from the park, in order to give the new generation of shrubs a promising start in life.

In the choice of shrubs I made what was, I suppose, a very obvious mistake. Naturally they had to be lime-tolerant, but I foolishly supposed that, since the Dell was so perfectly sheltered, rather delicate shrubs such as cistuses of various sorts, and *Veronica* (Hebe) *Headfortii* which I had seen ramping in Sir Edward Stern's chalk garden at Highdown, would feel perfectly at home there. Alas, I knew nothing of the katabatic propensity of frost, which billows down into this enclosed area, where there is neither an exit nor wind to disturb, and effectively exterminates all tender shrubs. So we turned to more robust plants such as *Juniperus Horizontalis*, the graceful fronds of which cover wide areas, *Viburnum Davidii* and *Tomentosum*, flowering cherries and deutzias; while at the bottom of the slopes where the soil is rather damp, astilbes, both pink and white, hostas, acanthus and so forth do well, and *Meconopsis Baileyi*, with some soil encouragement, makes a fair display. But the greatest summer effect is created by the Giant Hemlocks, which find the east-facing slope entirely to their liking, and push their huge leaves and tall stems topped by flat green flowers up amongst the shrubs and produce a scene almost suggestive of a tropical jungle.

As can be seen, there is nothing here of particular interest in itself, all the plants are commonplace and hardy, and the only virtue I can claim for the Dell is that full advantage has been taken of its unexpected contours, and that it forms an agreeable contrast to other parts of the garden.

The Garden II

The initial post-war work on the Dell represented to some degree rehabilitation, but as the years passed it became possible to carry out actual improvements. The shrub beds which, as I have already mentioned, were made during the winter of 1939/40, were still far from fully planted. It is an area which receives the full force of the south-west gales so that the beds on the windward side had to be treated primarily as wind-breaks. *Osmanthus Armatus*, the taller growing escallonias such as *langleyensis* and *edinensis*, berberis and so forth fulfil this function successfully, so that on either side of the main walk which leads down towards the old avenue we have been able to grow rather more interesting shrubs. Kolkwitzias flower well when the birds leave their buds alone, *Buddleia Alternifolia* grows into huge bushes, Cotinus, Philadelphus Beauclerk and Belle Etoile seem indifferent to the thin, poor soil. For smaller shrubs I find the evergreen Daphnes, *neapolitana* and *collina*, are successful and in addition to their neat growth have the happy habit of flowering twice a year.

At the point where the walk leads over a cattle-grid into the park we planted a pair of broad-leaved hollies, which have now grown into quite noble sentinels and form tall pyramids of shining, viridian foliage. Towards the front of the beds there are many low-growing plants: Pulmonarias of various varieties, Dicentras, the dwarf Polygonum and also *P. Campanulatum*, but a list of names becomes tedious, and I will here mention only one other ground-cover which is one I greatly regret having introduced. It is the yellow flowered creeping nettle, *Lamium Galeobdolon Luteum Variegatum*, which in this position spreads so luxuriantly that left to its own devices it would submerge all small plants and would even, I believe, throttle shrubs. It is difficult to eradicate, but every winter we treat it with the utmost violence digging it up and cutting it back ruthlessly and so prevent it from becoming too grave a menace. The pink-flowered Lamium is far better behaved, and also much more attractive with its neat, variegated leaves.

Now that the shrubs have reached maturity the eye is well guided down the walk and the avenue beyond. To provide a classical note to the scene a few years ago I erected at the end of the avenue a stone obelisk about 12 feet in height, while at the top, on the north side of the long walk, I built a small temple with a pillared front supporting a pediment. Within the temple I placed a porphyry bust of Poppaea, Nero's second wife, who like his first, Octavia, came to an unhappy end. The difference in the axes of the Tudor and the Georgian house here becomes very apparent. The path continuing the line of the old avenue joins the long walk at an oblique angle, so that the little temple, which had of course to be set at the upper end of the former and also parallel to the latter, seems to look away slightly to the west in rather a haughty manner instead of gazing directly at the obelisk. Fortunately slight irregularities in a garden seem to matter very little.

Adjacent to the temple grows a large bush of *Cotinus Atropurpureus*, which in this chalky soil colours well, and its deep crimson leaves contrast attractively with the stone pillars and grey and white paint of the little building. Further east along the walk is a large bed of grey-leaved Cotoneaster. It was grown from seed sent from Wisley many years ago and is, I think, *Franchetti*, and now forms a rather striking group with its graceful, pendulous branches. Further along again, beyond the steps leading up to the former rose garden, is a semicircular bed of a different style. It is presided over by a large specimen of *Pyrus Salicifolia Pendula* which stands in front of a tall copper beech. In spring round the foot of the Pyrus grow wallflowers which scent the whole of this part of the garden, and for the summer and autumn pale yellow dahlias take their place. The russet-crimson of the tree, the silver of the Pyrus and the lemon-coloured flowers of the dahlias make a harmonious and effective colour scheme.

From this point one can ascend the flight of steps to the former rose garden where in the past, as I have already described, so many generations of hybrid teas spent their brief lives. I started alterations on this garden before the war. The ragged barricade of laurels which surrounded it was swept away, and in its place I planted a yew hedge to give this little garden architectural form. It is now rectangular except for the east side which ends in a wide curve. From the centre of the curve steps lead down towards the Dell, while the long flight southward to the long walk was rebuilt and widened. In a yew recess on the north side I placed a marble Roman bath, Roman in design that is to say, but probably eighteenth-century in execution. The expiring rose bushes were removed and in their place I indulge, contrary to the best contemporary taste, in bedding out—blue and pink polyanthus in spring and heliotrope in summer. Behind the surrounding hedge grow various varieties of philadelphus, tall-growing shrub roses, Crimson Bouquet, Fritz Nobis and Nevada for early summer, which are infinitely tougher than hybrid teas, with *Buddleia Davidii* for later in the season. I find it pleasant to see loose-growing plants appearing above the rigid lines of a well-clipped hedge.

I was very slow indeed in appreciating the charm of shrub roses, influenced perhaps by the failure of hybrid teas, and it was not until about 1950 when my friends Christopher and Betty Hussey took me in June to Sissinghurst Castle that their overwhelming beauty dawned on me. I was further encouraged by Miss Sackville-West assuring me that they were not fastidious about soil. That autumn I sent out a considerable order: it is a proceeding I have continued annually ever since.

There was what seemed to me an admirable situation for these roses. On the north side of the western section of the long walk was a wide slope which had been formed when the walk was levelled. It faced due south, which was propitious, and the fact that it was on one of the pockets of heavy clay was perhaps more promising than sheer chalk, which is apt to be the alternative in this difficult garden. In the event the strong roots of most shrub roses seem able to penetrate the clay, and after a year or two's growth they began to present a beautiful tumult of blossom. Rather lavish feeding, however, seems essential, and we find that in this cold clay they have a tendency to become woody and gaunt, so that annual cutting out of old wood is essential.

At the top of the slope we planted taller varieties, so that their flowers can be seen from the house above the yew hedge which borders the terrace. Frühlingsgold, William Lobb, Zephyrine Drouhin, and her near relative Kathleen Harrap, Madame Isaac Pereire, all look well in this position, while towards the bottom of the slope are Penelope, Felicia, Rosa Mundi, Cornelia, Tuscany, Könegin von Dänemark, Alba Celestial . . . but the list is endless. Inevitably at the initial planting there were mistakes either in heights or juxtaposition of colours, so that a good deal of moving took place, while those varieties which are not successful we ruthlessly eliminate. We have added height to the border by erecting pyramids formed of larch poles, and on these we grow ramblers and climbers. After the first two years, during which the pyramids looked singularly gaunt, the effect is quite good, and the flowering season of the border is thus prolonged.

The Garden II

On the south side of the walk was a long bed filled with fairly tough shrubs designed to break the wind, but these have now in a large measure given way to more shrub roses, while the solid bushes serve as useful hosts for climbers. It cannot be said that the roses are as floriferous here as they are in the full sunshine across the path. Several years later, with unabated enthusiasm for roses, we decided to make a long, crescent-shaped bed on the south side of the sheltering shrubs where there was nothing to break the full force of the wind, but where also every ray of sunlight was obtained. This new venture has in fact been a success, but we find it prudent to train the roses over frames or on to low pyramids so that they are not unduly disturbed by a gale.

It is easy to ramble on about one's own garden supposing that one is transmitting the familiar scene to a reader, and that he will be forming a picture of the garden in his mind's eye. Probably, however, the only impression one is creating is one of boredom, so perhaps it will be wise to hasten past one or two features which are not of particular interest to describe, although they play an important part in the appearance of the garden and house.

I will, therefore, mention only briefly that there is a border which lies under the house and where sun-loving plants overflow on to the flagstones of the terrace. While below the low wall which retains this terrace is another long border which we have filled with small shrubs, interspersed with plants which need a sunny site, such as Mr. Lewis Palmer's hardy Agapanthus, Headbourne hybrids, both pale and dark blue, which here not only flourish but increase, Alstroemeria ligtu hybrids, which are slow starters but are worth waiting for, and *Hyacinthus Candicans*, and so on. The scenic advantage of these two borders is that together they form a leafy and mellow-coloured podium from which the house rises, its rigid lines softened by the double belt of foliage at its base.

Before the east end of the house extends a long formal pool, its stone surround centred on the middle of the five windows of the drawing-room. In order to give perfect symmetry to the surrounding lawn we made a long bed on the south side now filled with the floribunda rose Iceberg, encircled by a narrow sea of mauve violas. The whole of this layout takes the place of my father's croquet lawn, and I am inclined to doubt whether he would consider it an improvement.

From this cursory survey of the area close to the house, I would like to pass on to, and to describe a little more at length, that part of the garden lying to the north. I have always admired country houses where, in the proper eighteenth-century style, the park on the entrance side comes up to the very walls of the house, and the garden is kept in an exclusive manner out of sight of arriving strangers. At Hinton, unfortunately, there is none of this dignified reserve, and the garden surrounds the house as it might do at a modest villa. This may be partly due to the moving of the site of the house: in any case it is a limitation I must accept.

On the Tithe Map of 1839 the site of the Tudor house is shown as an enclosure marked 'Old House Site', and perhaps it was used as a little meadow. For as long as I can remember, however, it has been an orchard, and as such it remains. When I was very young it was surrounded by a thorn hedge, but this was long ago removed and my mother planted quantities of daffodils under the fruit trees, which make a pretty show in spring as one arrives at the house. The apple trees, it must be owned, have never been highly successful, probably because their roots have to force their way amongst brickbats and the remains of the foundations of the old house. Nevertheless they made an exquisite display when in blossom—and what blossom is more lovely—but, alas, the bullfinches have, anyhow for the present, put an end to this, and '*Le vert retour du doux Floréal*', as Verlaine puts it, is no longer celebrated with clouds of pink and white petals. As compensation we make the trees into useful hosts for *Rosa Filipes*, Kiftsgate var., whose flowers drip from the branches which rarely produce blossom of their own.

Across this orchard we have made two wide mown paths crossing at right angles. The east to west section is centred at one end on the tall iron gate into the kitchen garden, and on the other, by chance, on to a little Gothic door into the church vestry. On either side of this path we planted borders of Phlox, which should have looked pretty in the dappled light and shade of the fruit trees in late summer. But they were a failure, a dead failure, and we came to the conclusion that the soil must be so impregnated with eelworm that all attempts to eradicate it would continue to fail. Now low box hedges have taken the place of these herbaceous plants.

The south–north path is bordered with beds of irises. These are certainly more rewarding than the Phlox, but they do not make a luxuriant annual display in the way that I had hoped. But the principal purpose of this path is to lead across the orchard to an area of the garden where the soil is really good. Before the war I had planted here a grove of beech trees and *acer platanoides* with the intention that when they grew tall they would give added shelter to the house from the north. Having made our iris walk we decided to continue the path into the grove and curve it westward so as to emerge through the avenue of yews which extends the line of the north drive.

Having had the soil analysed, we found to our delight that it was almost lime-free, the chalk subsoil being covered with a very deep layer of good loam. Obviously it was worth while trying here plants which were reluctant to thrive in other parts of the garden. Having removed a number of the young trees to let in light, we started off with Magnolias, *liliflora nigra, Wilsonii*, and *Highdownensis*, and this gave an excuse for calling this new area, since all parts of a garden must have some designation, the Magnolia Garden. It is grandiose in name, but small in extent.

In the company of the magnolias we planted, with some apprehension, a few Exbury Hybrid Azaleas, pinks and yellow, but no orange, and these so far do well, as does a group of rhododendrons with glaucous leaves and small mauve flowers. Inevitably we had to try Camelias, one of the most beautiful of shrubs, but they grow very slowly and flower sparsely, and I feel ashamed of them when I see huge, noble bushes in localities that are really congenial to them. Hydrangeas of various sorts do well, and *Primula Candelabra* enjoy the rather damp soil and make a good spring show. Many other plants grow here with great exuberance, and I feel constantly how effortless gardening must be for the fortunate ones whose whole gardens are on soil such as this.

There is only one other feature which I propose to mention, and this is the shrub border lying between the drive and the kitchen garden. For many years there was here a herbaceous border, and with the high wall of mellow brick behind it, it was admirably placed. But it needed more attention than we could give it, and usually before the summer was half over it was almost submerged beneath a cloak of convolvulus and bindweed. The obvious solution was to abandon plants for shrubs, but in order properly to replace the herbaceous border it was necessary to have shrubs which flowered late in the summer, and this was not entirely easy, but on the whole we have been tolerably successful. At the back are tall-growing Hydrangeas, *aspera macrophylla* I think, and Velosa; *Buddleia Davidii*, of which we find Charming the most effective variety, throws out its mauve-pink spikes and contrasts well with the exquisite deep blue of *Ceonothus Topaz*. *Escallonia Iveyi* is useful in the back row, and *Hibiscus Woodbridge* and *sinosyriacus* are effective in a favourable summer. Indigoferas have a long but never very showy flowering season, and Fuchsias, par-particularly the sturdy Mrs. Popple, and Potentillas are invaluable in the front. In general the colouring tends towards mauves and blues and this effect is increased by the many Clematis entwined with the climbing roses on the wall behind the shrubs.

On the whole it can be said that the garden is fairly easy of upkeep, although there are large areas of mowing to be done each week in summer, and very, very many yards of hedge to be clipped annually. But shrubs, supported by ground-cover, entail much less work than herbaceous borders, and repay generously the attentions of feeding and pruning.

The Park

The improvements to the surroundings of Hinton have not been confined only to the garden: they have also been extended outwards into the park and have even embraced some areas of the adjacent landscape.

I have the impression that the Tudor house may have had a fairly extensive park, but when it was replaced by the Georgian house, which was little more than a shooting box, the park was curtailed and the timber cut. Certainly the 25 or 30 acres of grassland studded with ancient trees was quite adequate to the size of the house. But when my grandfather transformed it into a Victorian mansion the surroundings were woefully out of scale with the new splendours. This, I think, he perceived, and expanded the boundaries somewhat and planted a few trees.

Thus the park remained until just after the turn of the century when my parents made a new drive down the northern slope to the main road in the valley. I say my parents, but it was in fact my mother's undertaking for she had been bequeathed a sum of money by her father specially to be used on making some improvement at Hinton. The drive, with the not very attractive gate and lodge were the outcome of this fortunate bequest. The drive traversed, once it had left the neighbourhood of the garden, what were little more than two fields. A certain number of trees were planted to break the bareness, but not nearly on a lavish enough scale. During my father's lifetime I was allowed to add a little to this parsimonious afforestation, but it was not until a few years before the war that I was able to make plantations as I wished.

The plantations consisted of beech interplanted with softwoods, Scotch and larch, to act as nurses to the beech which are notoriously slow starters. During the six years of the war the trees were left to their own devices, and when I came to examine them in 1945 I found that the nurses, which had made exuberant growth, were fast suffocating and starving their little charges. I started to cut out the softwoods immediately, a certain number every year so as not to expose the beech too suddenly, but even so the beech took a year or two to recover from their wartime experiences. Eventually, however, vigour returned and they grew swiftly.

It is my intention that these little plantations shall not develop into clumps, but into groups of trees. That is to say that each tree shall keep its natural form. This entails, of course, constant thinning, a few trees every year. If I can achieve this, of which I am doubtful, each group will not only have the deep shadow created by the cattle-line, but there will also be shadows between the trees, and this will add greatly to the richness of the texture of the group.

In this I deviate from the principles advanced by Humphry Repton in his *Observations on the Theory and Practice of Landscape Gardening*. He advocated a casual style of planting as creating a natural and picturesque effect, and this, he explained, would be enhanced by trees which were in themselves poor specimens. These were his words:

> Those pleasing combinations of trees which we admire in forest scenery, will often be found to consist of forked trees, or at least of trees placed so near each other that the branches intermix, and by a natural effort of vegetation the stems of the trees themselves are forced from that perpendicular direction, which is always observable in trees planted at regular distances from each other. No groups will therefore appear natural unless two or more trees are planted very near each other.

I remain, however, unrepentant, much as I admire Repton's tenets in most directions, for misshapen trees in a park are anathema to me.

Rejecting Repton's advice, I have also planted a number of single trees, but once again in groups. They are mostly the usual park trees, limes, chestnut, both horse and Spanish, Norway Maples which turn a brilliant clear yellow in autumn, Turkey oaks which have a delicate foliage and elegant form; also a few plane trees which are not a success in spite of a good depth of soil on this northern slope. Thus this area is fast becoming well furnished, but another century will have to pass before it becomes an impressive park.

The area to the south of the house gave more scope for dramatic —modestly dramatic—planting for the lie of the land in the middle foreground was propitious for a scheme of this sort. As with the garden, I had the words of Alexander Pope constantly in mind, and the following verse was fairly applicable to what I hoped to achieve.

> *Consult the genius of the place in all;*
> *That tells the waters or to rise, or fall,*
> *Or helps th' ambitious Hill the heav'n to scale,*
> *Or scoops in circling Theatres the Vale,*
> *Calls in the country, catches opening glades,*
> *Joins willing woods, and varies shades with shades.*
> *Now breaks, or now directs, th' intending Lines,*
> *Paints as you plant, and as you work, designs.*

Needless to say these noble precepts were severely modified in my scheme, while the second line had no place in it at all, since only in the wettest of winters does a temporary lake appear in the valley. However, the middle foreground is highly important to the landscape as seen from the windows, and its proper planting greatly enhances the panorama of down-like hills which rises beyond the groves of trees which encircle and hide the village of Kilmeston in the middle distance.

When I began my operations the southern slope of the park was bounded, at little more than 200 yards from the house, by a wide row of hazel and sundry elm trees, which ran along the top of the steep bank marking the parish boundary. At the bottom of the bank was, and still is, a grass track on the line of the ancient highway from Winchester to Petersfield. Beyond the track the slope rises and undulates towards Kilmeston. It was criss-crossed with hedges, which obscured its contours, but was bare of all trees except for a copse on the west side. It was in fact a very bleak area.

The first task was to remove the hazel row and the indifferent elm trees; by this means the view from the house was opened on to the opposite slope. On the summit of the rise I persuaded my father to allow the planting of a wide belt of beech trees, thus, in a humble way, helping 'th' ambitious Hill the heav'n to scale'. It was necessary to take a long view, for on this very chalky ridge the trees have been slow to grow; but now, forty years later, they achieve the effect of making the rise seem higher than it is. At a later date all the distracting hedges were removed, and the eye is now directed by the presence of the beech belt on one side and the copse on the other along a shallow valley into the groves of trees in the middle distance.

Along the lane on the west side I planted an avenue of beech, which thickens at one point into a plantation, while a belt of beech was planted on two sides of a meadow on the west effectively furnishing this area. On either side of the slope we made two large plantations of mixed trees, chestnut, beech, Norway maple, roughly circular in shape and these, like those on the north side, will eventually appear as groups of trees and not clumps. Though still far from full-grown, they already cast long morning and evening shadows across the undulations of the grassland and have converted a bleak and barren slope into something of beauty, while the changing colours of their foliage add greatly to the interest of this middle foreground.

Index

Index

Books in National Trust Classics

Bath
Edith Sitwell
A lively and unorthodox look at the development of Bath from the arrival of Beau Nash in 1702 to the end of the century, concentrating on Bath society, written in 1932.

The Earls Of Creation
James Lees-Milne
The five Earls who are the subject of this book flourished at a time when the amateur exercised great influence over taste. Burlington, Pembroke, Leicester, Oxford and Bathurst created superb domains, most of which are still standing unaltered today.

Felbrigg, The Story of a House
R.W. Ketton-Cremer
Introduction by Wilhelmine Harrod
First published in 1962, this memoir is the history of a Norfolk country house from the 17th century until the 1960s, and the four families who have lived there. Written by one of the last members of the Ketton-Cremer family who bequeathed the house to the National Trust in 1969, the book pays tribute to this great house and its traditions.

First And Last Loves
John Betjeman
Illustrations by John Piper
An exuberant, convivial and affectionate collection of

essays in which Betjeman writes very much as he was wont to speak, considering examples of architecture from Cheltenham to Leeds, London's railway stations to Ilfracombe's summer residences.

Gallipot Eyes
A Wiltshire Diary
Elspeth Huxley

An evocative diary of village life in a small Wiltshire community by the well-known author of *The Flame Trees of Thika*. Elspeth Huxley's diary records her everyday preoccupations, describes the people round her and notes the ever-changing patterns of existence.

Ghastly Good Taste
Or, a depressing story of the Rise and Fall of English Architecture
John Betjeman

Ghastly Good Taste is Betjeman's witty and often irreverent guide to the history of architectural taste, in which he works his way through from the beauty of the Gothic period to the 'horrors' of the 1930s, with his distinctive narrative flair and gift of the unexpected evident throughout.

The Housekeeping Book of Susanna Whatman
Susanna Whatman
Introduction by Christina Hardyment

As Mistress of Turkey Court, Kent, Susanna Whatman wrote down detailed household instructions for her servants, giving a fascinating picture of life 'below stairs' in an 18th-century house.

The Rule of Taste
John Steegman
Introduction by Gavin Stamp
First published in 1968, Steegman's entertaining book traces the various changes in the arts of gardening, architecture and painting from the early 18th century to the early 19th century.

Uppark And Its People
Margaret Meade-Fetherstonhaugh and Oliver Warner
Introduction by Martin Drury
An entertaining portrait of life over three centuries in the late 17th-century house of Uppark, built high on the Sussex Downs and now one of the National Trust's most highly regarded houses of its period.

Victorian Taste
John Steegman
Foreword by Sir Nikolaus Pevsner
First published in 1980 as *Consort of Taste 1830–70*, *Victorian Taste* tackles the period covering twenty years on either side of the Great Exhibition, and includes lively portraits of key figures.

The Wild Garden
William Robinson
Introduction by Richard Mabey
The Wild Garden, published in 1870, has had a profound influence on gardening thought and theory, and has never been more topical than today, when so many of our wayside and woodland flowers are being lost to urban development and insecticides. In it William Robinson attacks the formal artificiality of high-Victorian gardens and passionately advocates the planting of wild and native flowers.